ZACH HUNTER

GENERATION CHANGE
Roll Up Your Sleeves and Change the World

ZACH HUNTER
FOREWORD BY WESS STAFFORD

GENERATION CHANGE
Roll Up Your Sleeves and Change the World

 ZONDERVAN®

ZONDERVAN.com/
AUTHORTRACKER
follow your favorite authors

invert

youth
specialties

Generation Change: Roll Up Your Sleeves and Change the World
Copyright 2008 by Zach Hunter

Youth Specialties resources, 300 S. Pierce St., El Cajon, CA 92020 are pub-
lished by Zondervan, 5300 Patterson Ave. SE, Grand Rapids, MI 49530.

ISBN 978-0-310-28515-1

Web site addresses listed in this book were current at the time of publi-
cation. Please contact Youth Specialties via email (YS@YouthSpecialties.
com) to report URLs that are no longer operational and replacement URLs
if available.

Cover design by SharpSeven Design
Interior design by David Conn

Printed in the United States of America

08 09 10 11 12 13 • 16 15 14 13 12 11 10 9 8 7 6 5 4 3

Dedicated to Jesus,
who showed us how to
love the poor

Contents

FOREWORD

I am always on the lookout for voices that will speak God's heart to a new generation. Zach Hunter is one of those voices. I am so encouraged when I hear young people not only speaking to their own generation, but also seriously challenging those of us who have gone before them. Zach articulates a high-definition message about a hurting world, but he also encourages us by zooming in on stories about people, groups, and ideas that actually make a difference. What's more, Zach helps us see that our battles aren't just "out there," they are also "in here"—deep in the chasms of our hearts. That's why issues of justice and compassion aren't add-ons for young Christians to consider. They are natural extensions of women and men who seek to walk in the footsteps of Jesus and to love as he loved. *Generation Change* challenges us to roll up our sleeves and open our hearts, and equips us to think creatively to make life better for those in desperate need.

Dr. Wess Stafford
President and CEO
Compassion International

BEFORE WE GET STARTED

I've had the privilege of meeting and talking with some of the most amazing people in the world. Some are famous—and others aren't but should be. These people are artists, activists, businesspeople, ministers, politicians, and everyday folks. All of them have made an impact on my life and the lives of those in need. To me, they are all heroes. Some have remained unthanked in their quiet duties, but not anymore. I would like to thank:

My dad, my mom, and my brother, Nate. Thanks for putting up with me, encouraging me, and giving me a place where I can be myself. I love y'all.

I'm grateful for the people who continue to teach me about God and his love for this messy world. Jon Foreman—for helping shape my thinking about the intersection of art and faith, for illuminating the dignity of the poor, and for carving out time for me; Dr. Wess Stafford from Compassion International—for teaching me that, in God's view, the poor are royalty; Corey Carnill—it's a privilege to be able to tell your story; thanks for trusting me with it.

There are many people who have stuck their necks out and taken a chance on a kid like me, people who have given me a platform to share what God's placed in my heart, and I owe all of you a huge debt—among others, you include Joel Houston, Paul and Andi Andrew, Brooke Fraser, JD, Phil Dooley and the whole Hillsong United gang, Steve Carter, Justin Mayo and Redeye Inc., Grace Neslon, John Ortberg, Jay Hein, and Jedd Medefind.

I also really appreciate the continued support of the Youth Specialties and Zondervan staff—Mark Oestricher, Jay Howver, David Welch, Roni Meek, Doug Davidson, Jeanne Stevens, and the rest of the crew. Thanks to Holly Sharp for a great cover design, and to Daley Hake for making everyone look so great in the photos! By the way, the cover shot is of "real" people: Christian Turner, Kendall White, Garrison Smith, Akil Mills, and Cory Rodgers—thanks for participating!

To Leeland "plural" and Darryl LeCompte for being like the big brothers I never had, and the whole Mooring family for praying for and supporting me. Speaking of prayer, I am very aware that many of you reading this book have prayed for me and I'm confident that through your prayers I have been encouraged and also protected from things I will never know of. Thank you. Thanks also to my prayer warriors, the Broas, Parva, Schulze, and Rehfeld families. Joel and Rachel Bennett (and Zion), thanks for great conversations and for putting up with me. Thanks also to Alex, Brett, and the Rebelutionaries for helping me see the advantages of rebelling against low expectations.

There are also a few people I've had the privilege of meeting in the past year who are heroes who have inspired me by facing personal struggles with great courage. Thanks to Robyn Roberts (for her contagious confidence); Danilo, Minnie, and Daniel Broas for proving God's goodness in the face of pain and illness; and Pat Padraja (keep going, little bro!)

Thanks to my church family at Grace Fellowship including Pastor Buddy, Randy Rainwater, Kenny Schmitt, and Aaron Keyes. I also want to thank the many youth pastors I have been able to meet this year who believe in Generation Change and have given themselves to see my generation become all God has planned for us.

And thanks to the many others who, by their creative work, advice, and the generous gift of your time have inspired me, including David Bean, Sara and Troy Groves, Dan Haseltine, Randy Alcorn, Stephen Christian, Darren Elder, and all the other artists who have made an impact in my life. Thanks also to Rich Van Pelt, Suzie Johnson, and the Compassion Family; Cheryl Noble from IJM; Kevin Bales, Peggy Callahan and Jolene Smith from Free the Slaves; and the many other people who have dedicated their lives to serving in the nonprofit world so others can have hope.

There's joy in serving, and we can often learn more about ourselves when we serve with friends. These are some of my friends from school who have supported my LC2LC campaign and who volunteer in many missions projects at school.

CHAPTER 1

Change Begins Here

> *"We're too young to know that some things are impossible, so we will do them anyway."*
>
> William Pitt in the film *Amazing Grace*

I'm really glad you picked up this book. Its purpose is to shed a little light on some of the biggest problems facing our generation and to inspire people to find ways they can make a difference. I'm only 16, and I don't pretend to be an expert on all these issues, but I'm learning a lot about the work that needs to be done. If you're an adult reading this, you may think, "He's so naive." Well, you're probably right...but I hope since I'm still just a teenager, you'll allow me to be naive for a little while longer.

As I've traveled I've met so many students who want to invest their youth to help improve the world.

I've been really inspired by my generation—not only by the encouragement other students offer me in my own efforts but the way so many kids in our generation are unselfishly helping others.

As you read this book, you'll notice I talk quite a bit about my faith. That might bother you if it isn't what you expected when you picked up the book. It's important for me to talk about how the life of Jesus and the Bible's teachings have shaped the way I view my responsibility in the world. But I know the big issues in this book are important to lots of people, not just Christians. So whether you share my beliefs or not—if you're interested in making a difference in this world, I welcome you. Thanks for reading.

In this book, you won't find a complete description of all the ins and outs of every issue or an exhaustive listing of every possible thing you can do to make an impact. What you *will* find is an overview, lots of ideas to get you going, and some personal stories of people from our generation who are working to change the world.

WHERE IN THE WORLD DO WE START?

We have to start with ourselves. We must undergo a change. We need a change in our thinking, a deeper commitment to helping "others," and maybe even a new sense of wonder about what could be and how we can be a part of making that happen. Ultimately, the change needs to happen within our hearts. For those of us who call ourselves Christians, that means seeking God diligently and yielding ourselves to him, asking him to change us and give us a new set of priorities and a deeper love for all people.

If we're really going to follow Jesus, we need to make sure our priorities are in line with his priorities. Over the past few years I've been amazed at the amount of teaching in the Bible that focuses on how we are supposed to treat the poor. I had no idea what a huge priority this was to God.

People sometimes say those of us who claim to follow Jesus are self-centered and focused on our own comfort and wishes. They think Christians seem petty and small-minded. It bothers me that some people may view me and my friends who follow Jesus in this way—especially since that's so far from what God calls us to be. I was just reading in the ancient book of Isaiah and discovered an interesting section where God talks about his priorities:

> "Is not this the kind of fasting I have chosen:
> to loose the chains of injustice
> and untie the cords of the yoke,
> to set the oppressed free
> and break every yoke?
> Is it not to share your food with the hungry
> and to provide the poor wanderer with shelter—
> when you see the naked, to clothe him,
> and not to turn away from your own flesh and blood?
> Then your light will break forth like the dawn,
> and your healing will quickly appear;
> then your righteousness will go before you,
> and the glory of the Lord will be your rear guard.

Then you will call, and the Lord will answer;
you will cry for help, and he will say: Here am I.
If you do away with the yoke of oppression,
with the pointing finger and malicious talk,
and if you spend yourselves in behalf of the hungry
and satisfy the needs of the oppressed,
then your light will rise in the darkness,
and your night will become like the noonday."

That's from the 58th chapter of Isaiah (vv. 6-10). I know it's kind of a long passage, but I hope you didn't skip it. If you did, please go back and read it. It's pretty radical. God says that if we spend ourselves on behalf of the hungry, and if we focus our attention on taking care of the poor, the hurting, and the oppressed, then we will shine. I think people who shine and reflect the goodness of God might be an answer to the criticisms many make about Christians.

WHY US?

I have a lot of hope in my generation. I really believe God wants to use us in incredible ways. Our generation has seen the hurting in the world in living color. The media has brought every major human rights, health, and environmental crisis right into our living rooms. We know the comfortable lifestyles of most Americans are not "reality" for most people in the rest of the world.

I'm writing this book near the end of 2007—the 40th anniversary of the famous "Summer of Love" that marked the beginning of the hippie movement. I believe our generation should launch a new movement of peace, love, and justice—but this time, do it with God. The hippies talked a lot about "free love," but we've got to realize that true, lasting, life-changing love isn't free. It costs—a lot! Real love means sacrificing something of ourselves, some of our own comfort. It means giving ourselves up like Jesus did. He wasn't prideful—even though he had all the answers. He wasn't a finger pointer—even though he was sinless. But he spoke the truth, even when the truth was hard to hear, and he got busy helping broken people put their lives together and meeting real needs like the need for food, shelter, and healing.

It's easy to complain about what's wrong with the world today. But I think my generation is tired of hearing complaints and excuses, and we're eager to see people get busy and do something about the problems. And I don't mean just more talking and meeting about the problems—I mean finding solutions to meet the needs. I think my generation feels a connection with history, rather than a hatred of it. We want to continue the good work that's being done, but also to write new chapters that show we've learned from some of the things done well (and done poorly) in the past. If we can learn from the failures and successes of those who have come before us, and work with God, we will not be stopped. We can carry on the torch of great people of the past. Who knows, maybe God has called this generation specifically to demonstrate his love and care for the poor? Maybe that is the work he's "prepared in advance for us to do (Ephesians 2:10)."

That's an exciting thought!

People sometimes talk about how the church is selfish. They say we're eager to build huge buildings and bigger parking lots, serve up fancy coffee and sit in cushy chairs, and stock the youth rooms of our churches with Wiis, Xbox 360s, and snacks—but ignore a hurting world. It's time to give people a different idea of what the church is all about. We hear a whole lot about what Christians are against (we're known for being "anti-this" and "anti-that")—and I do think it's important to stand against some things.

> **"Each person must live their life as a model for others."**
>
> Rosa Parks

But it's time for a generation of Christians who are known because they stand up for something. It's time for a new day. It's time for *Generation Change*.

So, if you're ready, here's what I think Generation Change would look like:

- People who love Jesus radically, and who translate that love into real action in their own lives and the lives of others.

- People who know that to love Jesus well, you need to know him personally and study his ways.

- People who demonstrate the love of Jesus by seeking to work shoulder to shoulder with all who share the desire to help others, not just with other Christians.

- People who lead humbly by serving.
- People who spend time helping the poor and the oppressed in the world.
- People who invest their influence to help others rather than hoarding it for themselves.
- People who prepare well for their future, so they are equipped to bring about change.

I've listed some of the poster children for Generation Change in my acknowledgments. I encourage you to check them out. These are people I am watching and learning from.

A youth worker once asked me, "If you could tell adults anything, speaking from your generation to ours, what would it be?" I had two things: The first had to do with our dreams. When speaking to kids, pastors and youth workers love to quote 1 Timothy 4:12: "Don't let anyone look down on you because you are young, but set an example for the believers in speech, in life, in love, in faith and in purity." My generation hears it all the time, but do we really believe it? Adults, imagine a kid walks into your office and says, "Here's my dream." The kid goes on to tell you about a ridiculously impossible plan for ending world hunger. What do you say? Would it be something like,

"Maybe when you're older." Or "Umm…right…but there are a few reasons why this isn't a good idea" or "That's been tried before, and it didn't really work that well." Or do you instead encourage that kid to pursue the dream and tell him how awesome it is that he wants to do something to help others rather than just thinking about himself? I encouraged the youth worker to let those kinds of dreams take root in kids' lives. Let them imagine the big things they might accomplish in the world. The time will come when they'll need you to talk through their plans and guide and direct them—but don't be quick to squash the dream with all the reasons you think it's unrealistic.

The second thing I told this youth worker was to give us God. My generation is dying of thirst in a desert and we don't even know there's an oasis right in front of us. We come to youth group and church because we think there may be answers there that we're not finding elsewhere. Sometimes instead of the living water Jesus offers, we're greeted with more of the same stuff we get the rest of the week—games, music, food—but very little God. I like fun and games, too—I *am* still a teenager—but I believe we're desperate for so much more. We don't need a fun and easy substitute. What we really need is to find our true identity and purpose in God and his teachings.

BEING GENERATION CHANGE

This book is intended to help equip Generation Change to get busy. Lots of people tell me their hearts are stirred to bring hope and help, but they aren't sure where to begin. If that's true for you, then you'll find some ideas in the pages ahead. Take them, expand on them, work them out in your community, make them better, and come up with your own.

A lot of the ideas in the book focus on helping children. I've learned children are often the most vulnerable people in the world, especially when they are orphaned. I've spent the last few years trying to work against modern-day slavery. (You'll read more about that in the chapter on Justice.) Once when I was taking questions after speaking to a group of students, a girl asked if adults were still enslaved today—because I'd been talking mainly about children in slavery. I responded that there are many adults enslaved today, but I tend to talk more about children for a couple of different reasons. First, since I'm a young person, the issue became more personal for me when I learned about kids my age in slavery. Second, half of all victims of slavery worldwide are children. And third, God has a soft spot in his heart for children. Jesus once said, "See that you do not look down on one of these little ones. For I tell you that their angels in heaven always see the face of my Father in heaven" (Matthew 18:10). Children are very close to the heart of God.

NEAR AND FAR

Some of the ideas you'll read about in this book are "near"—they're about addressing problems in your own neighborhood. Some are "far" away—in other parts of the world. You may not be able to travel all over the world, but you can raise money and awareness, and through those activities you can bring help to the people who live far away. I think we need to balance the two—helping neighbors near and far.

Hey, I want to thank you again for reading through this book and for walking with me on this journey. I'm learning a lot. At times I'm disappointed in myself and my walk with Jesus. I feel discouraged by how much I have to learn and the opportunities I miss to make the most of what I do know. But more often I'm excited at the possibility of being used by God. I feel like I'm getting to know him better. And I'm thrilled to be a part of a generation of young people who are coming together to make our world a better place.

I hope we can continue to learn together how to spend ourselves on behalf of the poor and be the Generation Change that will spark a revival that transforms the world.

Students spent the night in their cardboard shacks and learned more about the lives of homeless people in their community during their Shack-a-Thon event.

CHAPTER 2

SHELTER

> *"The world is full of suffering. It is also full of overcoming it."*
>
> Helen Keller

Billy is 10 years old. His dad ran out on the family when Billy was just a baby, so he never knew his father. The other kids in his fourth-grade class won't play with him because they say he smells bad. But they have no idea what Billy's life is like...

Children can be cruel. Billy knows this well. Even his teacher misunderstands why his father can't come to school events. She thinks Billy lies to her—and he does, but that's because she can't know. No one can find out. He figures it's a good thing she doesn't try harder to find out what's going on.

Even if his teacher wanted to know more, Billy wouldn't tell her. And so, day after day, he carries this weight, his secret, around inside him. At times, it seems heavier than he can bear, like he might collapse under the load of this dark, depressing burden.

He can't even describe what he feels—what it's like to live in his neighborhood. Just last Thursday he saw that girl walking down his street—the girl in his class with the pigtails and the shining smile. But Billy didn't say anything to her as she walked by. He knew she couldn't stand him, couldn't *understand* him... because she didn't know what it is like. She doesn't know what it's like to have someone walk right by you on the street and pretend you aren't there. It's even worse when someone *does* notice you and gives you that pitiful look—the look people have when they see an injured animal on the side of the road.

Billy doesn't want pity, he wants love. He wants a place where he belongs. Billy is homeless.

Can you imagine yourself in Billy's situation? Most of us can't. Most of us take it for granted that we have a roof over our heads, three meals a day, more than one pair of jeans and two shirts, a pantry where we can go grab a snack anytime we want, and even deodorant. Imagine a world where you have no TV, no iPod, no means of transportation, and no warm shower. Imagine being afraid to get too close to anyone, never being able to tell anyone where you lived, because if you were telling the truth, the answer would be... *nowhere*.

When you hear the word *shelter*, you might immediately think "homeless shelter." But that's not all I'm talking about. I'm talking about shelter as a place that's indoors, away from the elements. Most of us spend so much time indoors that the concept of not having an "indoors" is odd to us. For many around the world there is no indoors. Life is completely lived outside. This leaves people more vulnerable to many things including dangerous weather, harsh elements, violence, and robbery. Tragically, many people live without shelter today in conditions that are much more severe and difficult than those faced by homeless people in our own nation. It's hard to believe, but true.

MORE THAN ENOUGH

Most of us have a lot of "stuff" in our houses—furniture, entertainment, food, decorations. What if we didn't have any of those? It's hard for me to even imagine something like that. Most of us don't have to pray that God would give us "enough"—instead we've been blessed with more than enough. What if we didn't have all the luxuries or even the bare necessities? American students often compare the size of their bedrooms, or brag about having rooms outfitted with TVs or computers or all sorts of other cool things. Yet many other people don't even have a safe place to live.

A couple of years ago my family made a decision to "downsize" our house. We had much more than we needed, more than my parents felt good about, and much more than we could take care of. My mom and I were talking about this recently, and we concluded that a lot of us in the Western world might need to start asking, "How little can we get by with?" instead of "How much more can we acquire?" I'm not saying I'm there yet, but I think the question is worth pondering.

It may be uncomfortable for us to think about, but many people go without the things we enjoy in our day-to-day lives. Those of us who do have enough should be doing something to help those who don't. In addition to folks who are completely without a home, there are many others living in houses in various states of disrepair. Sometimes the houses are actually dangerous. There is one situation in particular I'd like to tell you about.

CHANGE IT: A HOUSE FOR JEN

I was speaking at a youth event in Nashville, and I walked by a display table with a banner that said "Build a House for Jen" (not her real name). The organizers of this conference had invited me to speak, hoping I could inspire their students to go do something important with their lives—but the inspiration, for me at least, was already there.

There were three teenage guys standing at that table who'd started this project called A House for Jen. Jen was a local girl who'd been born with a disability that left her unable to walk. She was living with her mom in a small house that was literally falling apart around them. They didn't even have a car, so Jen's mom had to push her wheelchair wherever they needed to go.

Now, these three guys were the type of guys you'd expect to be the captains of the football team. They were athletes, people everyone looked up to, popular kids. They chose to befriend Jen and spend time with her. They met her where she was at—literally. These guys would go to her home, hang out with her, learn about her life and her needs. I think the picture we have of most "jocks" and popular kids in school is that they wouldn't give their time to do something like this—they wouldn't even want to be seen in her company. Not these guys. Because they were followers of Jesus, they didn't pick friends based on what someone had or a person's situation.

> *"I think a lot of us in the Western world might need to start asking, 'How little can we get by with?' instead of 'How much more can we acquire?'"*

When these guys realized Jen's home badly needed repair, they decided to try to fix it up themselves. So they started tackling one home-improvement problem after another, but the house was in such bad condition they really couldn't fix it anymore. They knew these little repairs weren't creating a long-term solution. After discussing it, they felt that if Jesus were in their situation, he would want to provide Jen and her mom with a new house. So they went to their church and asked for help to do exactly that. One woman donated the land, and the guys began raising money. Their goal is to raise enough to build the home Jen needs. I think that is so cool. They met a person who had a need, and they are using what they have to meet that need.

CHANGE IT: YOUR TURN

Like the guys above, you might know someone in your neighborhood, church, or community who could use some help with their shelter. You don't always have to go through an organization to provide help—maybe God wants to use you to directly impact someone in your community. Ask God to show you people in need and see how you can help. Maybe you could do work on their house, protecting it from cold winter weather, repairing dangerous situations, etc. Jen's friends could have called *Extreme Makeover: Home Edition* to build the new house for Jen, but then they would have missed out on the joy of being used by God. And they would have missed out on a growing friendship with Jen and her mom.

Nickels for Nails

On the youth section of the Habitat for Humanity Web site, you'll find the story of a fifth-grader who found out about Habitat and its work, and wanted to do something. This kid's name is Jacob Amaya, and he's helping lead a fundraiser at his elementary school. The project is called Nickels for Nails, and its goal is to fund 250 homes in Los Angeles, California, over a three-year period of time.

Shack-a-Thon

These "Shack-a-Thons" are held all over the country, but one group I learned about is in Litchfield, New Hampshire. They are proof you don't need a huge youth group to make a difference. The youth minister at St. Francis Parish wanted to help the kids there develop compassion for people who are homeless— a problem that is often invisible or ignored. She said, "I hoped that this event would help them appreciate their own blessings in life, and inspire them to share their wealth with others."

When the students arrived on the afternoon of the shack-a-thon, they were given cardboard and duct tape to begin constructing the "houses" in which they'd be sleeping that night. They had dinner, fellowshipped, celebrated Mass, had a time of prayer, and talked about the problems facing the homeless. They then slept in their "homes" for the night. Each of the students collected sponsorships from family and friends. This youth group raised more than $2,000 during their shack-a-thon. One of the girls, Courtney, raised $300 by herself.

The students were encouraged to think about this as a first step in identifying with suffering people and then looking for ways to get involved. Youth minister Jyl Dittbenner said, "I think that they will remember how uncomfortable it was to sleep in a box, that they will feel thankful for their own situations, and feel the urge to reach out to the larger community through their service and donations."

You can take this basic idea and expand upon it. Build a cardboard city on your church or school lawn. Write facts about homelessness on the side of the houses. Leave it up for a week and ask people to "buy" the houses or sponsor the students who will spend a night sleeping in the cardboard houses. The next morning you could even go to a homeless shelter to serve breakfast and deliver the funds to the director of the facility. Or you could make a giant check together and ship it to an organization that works on housing issues.

In the United States:

One out of every four homeless persons is a child.
(U.S. Department of Health and Human Services)

Twenty-five percent of all homeless persons are war veterans.
(U.S. Department of Health and Human Services)

One in four homeless persons is mentally ill.
(National Law Center on Homelessness and Poverty)

Habitat for Humanity

One of the things I love about Habitat for Humanity is the way the family who will receive the house that's built works alongside the volunteers to build the new home. Habitat has worked in more than 90 countries around the world.

According to the Habitat Web site, the cost of a home can be anywhere from $800 to $60,000, depending on the circumstances. Although it is a Christian organization, Habitat doesn't choose who to build houses for based on religion.

Your youth group might want to go on a Habitat "build" in your community, or you could bake cookies and take water to other volunteers who are building a Habitat home. You could also help furnish the home of a family who has become a first-time homeowner with Habitat's support. You must be at least 16 years old to build on a Habitat site, but there are other things you can do to get involved with Habitat for Humanity. Check out their Web site at www.habitat.org.

> **Other Organizations that help provide shelter:**
>
> World Vision www.worldvision.org
>
> Fuller Center for Housing www.fullercenter.org
>
> Association of Gospel Rescue Missions www.agrm.org
>
> Salvation Army www.salvationarmy.org

BRAINSTORM FOR CHANGE

- Build birdhouses or buy them from a craft store and have students paint and decorate them. Then have an auction to raise money for Habitat for Humanity, Salvation Army, or your local homeless shelter.

- Your group could team up with either students in an advanced woodshop class or a few adults with building skills to build playhouses. Then work with the local mall or a park to display them. Auction off the mini-houses to help build homes in your community.

- Have a recycling drive in which people in your community drop off furniture, toasters, washers and dryers, etc., in your church parking lot. Then distribute them to families in need. Our church is helping furnish homes of refugees moving into the area. This is a great outreach opportunity for any church.

- Recycle old wooden chairs that you can pick up at thrift shops or that others were going to throw away. Recruit teams of students to create cool, one-of-a-kind designs on the chairs using paint, decoupage, and other techniques. Then auction the chairs off at your school or church. These pieces of art would also provide a neat gallery exhibit where you could raise awareness about the problems of homelessness and poverty in your community.

- Perhaps your family could make a room in your home available for someone who is homeless or in need of transitional housing. This may seem like a radical idea, but just imagine what God could do!

Photo courtesy of: Free the
Slaves | Peggy Callahan

*Rambho's mom was tricked
into selling her child into
slavery after her husband
died. He has been free one
month in this photo. Workers at Bal Vikas Ashram,
where he is rehabilitating,
say it takes about three
months for the children to
learn to play again and for
their personalities to emerge
after years of abuse.*

CHAPTER 3

JUSTICE

"Without justice, there can be no peace. He who passively accepts evil is as much involved in it as he who helps to perpetrate it."

Dr. Martin Luther King Jr.

Justice has become the new buzzword for a lot of different activities in missions. I may have a narrower definition of justice than some other people, but I tend to think of it as righting or preventing a wrong against somebody—like freeing someone who's held captive, restoring a widow's land after it's been stolen, or requiring the people who cause an environmental mess to take responsibility for cleaning it up.

Injustice is everywhere. Oppressors thrive in situations where those who have the ability to step between the vulnerable and their abusers fail to do so. In some cases, this might mean law enforcement officers are involved in the crimes or taking bribes to look the other way. In other cases, people may choose to think the injustice is just not that bad, or they hope someone else will fix the problems.

Injustice takes on many ugly forms including the abuse of widows and orphans. In many countries greedy family members illegally strip the land from women whose husbands die. This is a huge problem in Africa where AIDS is leaving many widows without the assets they once shared with their husbands. Widows and orphans are also vulnerable to theft and exploitation by powerful people who want to extort money or belongings from them or abuse them in other ways.

In some parts of the world, parents sell their own children into brothels, or children and women are trafficked to be used as sex slaves after being kidnapped or falsely promised a good job to help their families. Once they arrive at the destination, the abuse escalates and they find themselves trapped, without identification and afraid for their lives. Injustice also occurs when men and women are wrongfully imprisoned or have their human rights violated because of their social standing, economic background, race, or nationality.

WHAT IS THE ANSWER TO INJUSTICE?

Some people look at the injustices of the world and say, "If there's a loving God, why does he let all this bad stuff happen?" Even Christians sometimes question how a loving God can allow all this suffering. Well, God loves the people of the world, and he wants to end the suffering. I know that for sure. In the words of Gary Haugen, president of International Justice Mission, "God has a plan to end the suffering in the world, and his plan is us!"

God loves justice. God hates injustice. God desperately wants to work with us to make this world a place of justice for all people. Sometimes I think God must feel like a father who is eagerly waiting for his son to come help him repair some problem in the house, but his son is too busy playing video games. Our loving God wants to be with us and partner with us to help others.

God is as passionate about seeking justice as he is about feeding hungry people. But I think justice can be a hard idea to wrap our little human minds around. It's easier to picture ourselves providing a meal for someone who is hungry than it is to picture what it would take to rescue a slave or free someone from prison.

> *"God wants to change the world with us and through us. But we need to be willing to risk something of ourselves."*

Maybe we're not in a place where we can do those things ourselves. Perhaps our role involves raising awareness, money, and political support to further the efforts of others working for justice in their own communities and contexts.

God wants to change the world with us and through us. But we need to be willing to risk something of ourselves. Our first step might be making ourselves open to having our hearts broken by the ugly truth of injustice. Then we need to ask: What do I have available to help right those wrongs?

CHANGE IT: FREE THE SLAVES

Those of you who know me or read my first book, *Be the Change*, already know that ending modern-day slavery is a huge priority for me. Several years ago, I learned that about 27 million people are held as slaves today, and I heard some of the specific stories of children who were oppressed and enslaved. At the time, I'd been studying history, and some of my greatest heroes were—and still are—abolitionists who worked to end slavery in the past. As I learned about modern-day slavery, I felt a strong desire to continue the work of these historical figures by fighting against slavery today. So I launched a campaign called Loose Change to Loosen Chains—a student-led effort to raise awareness and funds to help end slavery once and for all.

Slavery today is a bigger problem than it has ever been. I know it's hard to believe that in the "free world" of the 21st century, many people are not free to come and go, to work and play, to realize their dreams. But it's true.

The good news is that there are lots of good people and organizations working for a permanent end to all slavery. Since launching Loose Change to Loosen Chains, I've learned about many great organizations working to bring freedom from slavery. One abolitionist organization I highly recommend is called Free the Slaves. One of the things I love about this group is that it partners with other smaller organizations working around the world to free slaves. Free the Slaves uses its influence and access to funding to get needed resources to these smaller organizations, which may not have access to donors and grants.

I recently heard the story of a young boy named Rambho who was rescued by a partner of Free the Slaves. Here's the short version of his story from their Web site:

> *Rambho Kumar was rescued from a carpet loom in India where he was forced to work 19 hours a day with no pay. The loom owner and trafficker seduced Rambho's mother with promises that Rambho would go to school and send money home to the family. Rambho's father had just died, and his mother could not feed the family. She sent Rambho with the trafficker.*
>
> *When Rambho's fingers bled from overwork, the slave owner would dip them in oil and light a match to them. He wasn't allowed to play or go to school. He was never allowed to visit his family or leave the loom.*

Finally, Rambho was rescued by liberators that Free the Slaves works with on the ground. Today, Ramhbo is free, and he plans to help his mother find a house. He also wants to make sure no other children become enslaved.

"I want to go in my village and be a guard over there, and I think that if I get out of here then I'll be able to study and I'll be able to earn money."

It's estimated that more than 27 million people in the world are held in slavery.
(Free the Slaves)

There have been 48 million abortions in the United States since 1973.
(Christian Life Resources)

Rambho's story is told in a film called *Freedom and Beyond*. You can purchase it on the Web site www.freetheslaves.net.

CHANGE IT: YOUR TURN

Loose Change to Loosen Chains

This is the effort I started when I was 12 years old. Through storytelling and the collection of loose change, you can help end slavery. You can learn more about it and download the tools you need to get started at www.lc2lc.org.

Students for Life

On campuses throughout the United States, you'll find Students for Life chapters, where next-generation leaders work to preserve the dignity and sanctity of the life of preborn humans. Visit www.studentsforlife.org.

International Justice Mission

IJM works to fight oppression and injustice around the world. Students can get involved with IJM in many ways including raising awareness and funds, becoming a prayer partner, or preparing for a career in justice by interning with IJM. Check them out at www.ijm.org.

Children of the Light Dancers

These teens have used their talents as dancers to educate people about justice. They do a special concert called "Seek Justice." Maybe you have a talent of your own that can be used to raise awareness and funds. Learn more about these teens and get inspired at www.childrenofthelightdancers.org.

Love 146

This organization used to be called Justice for Children International. They renamed themselves in honor of a young girl they saw being sold who had been given a number (146) instead of being called by her name. On their Web site you'll find many ways to get involved in helping to free children from sex trafficking. Check it out at www.love146.org.

Voice of the Martyrs

At www.persecution.com you'll learn about modern-day martyrs and other people being persecuted for their faith. Find out how to get involved in defending people's right to worship and believe as they choose.

BRAINSTORM FOR CHANGE

- Justice Film Festival: Choose a film that tells the story of justice and get permission to show it for a group. Hold a film festival where people pay admission or make donations that are given to a justice-seeking organization. A few suggestions for films to purchase for the festival: *Freedom and Beyond, Bella, Amazing Grace,* or *Not for Sale.* You might even want to hold a film competition where students create their own films about justice issues.

- Solidarity Sunday: Hold a special worship service focused on injustices going on around the world. Have students all wear black T-shirts or arm bands to show solidarity with victims of oppression.

- Justice Dinner: I heard of a youth group that held a dinner to benefit IJM. The idea was something like this: Each person attending paid $10 for a meal. A very few of them were given steak dinners; a larger number of them were given rice, beans, and water; and the last group (the majority) were given bread and water. The students spoke at the dinner and explained how this represents the reality of injustice for many poor persons around the world. This was a powerful word picture for attendees.

• Justice Concerts: Bring in a band that has a heart for justice and hold a concert to raise money to end slavery or promote justice. Possible performers include Lamont Hiebert, Sara Groves, The Wrecking, Leeland, Braddigan, Ginny Owens, Shaun Groves, Derek Webb, or The Washington Project—artists who have all taken stands for justice and who sometimes do smaller events.

Justin Mayo lives a life of kindness whether reaching out to the homeless, caring for friends of the L.A. Dream Center, or investing in the lives of volunteers.

Justin leads a community of next-generation leaders in Hollywood as they find meaning and significance through serving others.

CHAPTER 4

KINDNESS

> *"Constant kindness can accomplish much. As the sun makes ice melt, kindness causes misunderstanding, mistrust, and hostility to evaporate."*
>
> Albert Schweitzer

A lot of the material in this book addresses massive global problems that have serious consequences. So kindness might seem trivial. But I wanted to include it because I think we have a shortage of kindness in Western culture today. You might even want to call it a kindness drought. And I think that has a huge effect on our world.

While responding to problems like hunger, homelessness, and the need for clean water might require significant planning and coordination, kindness is something we can practice every day. Kindness can become a habit that will improve not only the lives of those around us but also our own lives. A study conducted by the National Institutes of Health showed a direct connection between people being kind and their own happiness. Kindness is part of the fruit of the Spirit (see Galatians 5:22), yet I don't think most of us act it out consistently in our daily lives.

Drivers cut other people off in traffic—even when they're rushing to get into the church parking lot for the prized parking space. Students hurry through the lunch line and grab several desserts, leaving others without any. We let doors slam in one another's faces. We don't hold the elevator for someone with baggage. We don't ask for forgiveness when we've wronged someone else—instead we excuse our behavior and say the other person is too sensitive and needs to get over it.

We need to be kinder. *I* need to be kinder.

By showing kindness to others, we acknowledge that every person is created in the image of God and deserves to be treated as someone who matters. Ultimately, God's kindness toward us should move us to show kindness to others.

CHANGE IT: TOOTSIE ROLLS AND STARBUCKS

I have several friends who have really shown me what kindness is. For them, kindness is not just a "sometimes thing"—it is a habit. I believe their kindness is proof of God's Spirit living within them.

One of these people is my Uncle Ted—or TJ, as others call him. He's sort of an adopted uncle for me.

Uncle Ted is pushing 80 years old, but lives "younger" than most people my age. He's one of those people who's always giving and thinking about others. He loves Tootsie Rolls, and wants you to love them, too, so he gives them out liberally. Uncle Ted always wants to buy you ice cream wherever you go. In restaurants, he often tells the waiter or waitress, "Whatever they pay you, you're worth more." My dad says that whenever he went into Uncle Ted's office, Ted would look up and tell my dad, "The answer is 'yes.' Now what do you want?" He lives out kindness in his day-to-day life. I truly believe he'd do whatever he could to help someone—any-one. Man, I'd like to be like him.

> **"I think our generation needs to be deliberate about kindness."**

Some people think being "nice" is somehow not "manly." You know, it's the "no more Mr. Nice Guy" idea. Well, if *nice* is synonymous with *kind*, then I think these people have it all wrong. Kindness should be growing like crazy among God's people.

When I visited Hillsong Church in Australia, our host Joel Bennett modeled kindness for us. Joel graciously asked what my mom and I wanted to do while we were there, and then took us to all the points of interest in Sydney, and took us shopping for Australian candy and clothes. We had a lot of great experiences with Joel, and Joel and I had some great conversations about the Bible. He shared experiences with us, he helped us make memories, and he served us. His kindness and openness provided the grounds for a lasting friendship.

I have another friend named Justin Mayo. He's a twenty-something guy who lives in Los Angeles at the L.A. DreamCenter. The DreamCenter is a place where people can come in off the streets and start their lives over. Justin lives in the DreamCenter, but commutes to various places in the city to lead Red Eye, a ministry he started to reach out to young people involved in entertainment, fashion, and other culture-shaping communities in Hollywood to demonstrate love and acceptance to them. I think Justin wakes up in the morning (or maybe he just dreams all night) thinking of ways he can be kind to others. Whether it's paying for someone's drink at Starbucks or driving a guest around so he won't have to take a cab, Justin is all about serving, serving, serving. Justin had me out to speak to the group at Red Eye, and I'm privileged to partner with him in his ministry. After the event, there was food left over, so Justin walked up to this homeless man and introduced himself, shaking the guy's hand

A study on kindness showed that kind people experience more happiness and have happier memories.

Simply by counting acts of kindness for one week, people feel happier and more grateful.

(National Institutes of Health)

and asking him about himself. Then Justin offered the food to the guy.

Justin is one of the wildest, most amazing guys you'll ever meet. But he's also one of the kindest. Kindness just flows from him.

If kindness is something you really struggle with, ask God to help you empty yourself of your own desires and selfishness and fill you with his Spirit. Since kindness is a fruit of the Spirit, a life lived in step with God and his Spirit will produce more kindness.

CHANGE IT: YOUR TURN

I think our generation needs to be deliberate about kindness. Forget about the "random acts"—let's *plan* to be kind. Let's decide we want kindness to be a habit. This requires focusing less on our own wants and needs and more on those of other people. If we become a kinder generation, I think we'll see a huge shift in our homes, our schools, and our culture.

It might sound dramatic, but your kindness could even end up saving a life. Paying someone a little bit of respect and attention could mean the world to that person. Let's get started. What do you say?

BRAINSTORM FOR CHANGE

Okay, here are a few ideas for how you can make the world a better place by bringing a little more kindness. These ideas aren't earth-shattering, but that doesn't mean they aren't important. I'm sure you can come up with some of your own.

- Find one kind thing you can do this week for someone you struggle to get along with.

- Make a cup of coffee or tea for a member of your family tonight.

- Hold a door open for someone.

- Ask if you can help someone carry a heavy load. The person may decline, but just the offer will communicate kindness.

- When you visit a bank, grocery store, or other business, ask the people working there how they are doing, and let them know you appreciate their efforts.

- Compliment someone at your school who doesn't receive a lot of affirmation.

- Send a text message to tell a friend what you appreciate about him or her.

- Mow a lawn. Rake some leaves. Clean the bathroom. Without complaining or being asked.

Get more ideas at www.actsofkindness.org.

CHAPTER 5

POVERTY

> *"Poverty often deprives a man of all spirit and virtue; it is hard for an empty bag to stand upright."*
>
> Benjamin Franklin

Poverty either causes or adds to just about every other social ill discussed in this book. Poverty keeps people from getting a good education, which in turn keeps them from having a good job. Poverty is a main catalyst for slavery and human trafficking, because people feel trapped into selling themselves or their children to get money to survive. Poverty keeps people living on the streets without adequate health care or roofs over their heads.

People who have plenty of connections and resources (as in relationships and money) are far less likely to struggle personally with the issues in this book. They may deal with illiteracy, but they have the help of schools and other educational services. They may have health problems, but they can usually afford the care they need. If they are accused of a crime, they can afford legal counsel. Even the poorest Americans would seem relatively wealthy compared with the poorest people in other parts of the world. In the United States, many areas have free medical clinics for those who can't afford health care for themselves. Nearly every American has access to water that's drinkable. In fact, the toilets in most American homes use the same safe, drinkable water that flows through our faucets, while people in other parts of the world are dying because they have no access to uncontaminated water.

> "Be kind, very kind, to the suffering poor. We little realize what they go through. The most difficult part is not being wanted."
>
> Mother Teresa

Since poverty is often hidden in Western culture, it makes it hard for many of us to relate. We tend to avoid even the most poverty-stricken areas of our own cities, because we think they're the "bad areas" of town. So whether the poor are in another country, or on the other side of the tracks, we still consider them to be "over there." In this way, we have become either unaware of, or numb to, the poverty both within our country and around the world.

We need to open our eyes and begin to see the poor around us. If we don't purposefully identify ourselves with the poor and the hurting in the world, then it is hard to be a part of the solution. We must acknowledge that something is terribly wrong in the world, and we can fix it. We cannot be afraid of seeing suffering, because the God whom we represent is stronger than the pain of what we see. Instead of turning a blind eye to poverty and pain, let's look it right in the face and ask, "What can we do?"

Deuteronomy 15:11 says, "There will always be poor people in the land. Therefore I command you to be openhanded toward your brothers and toward the poor and needy in your land." If you walked up to a few random people, and asked them to describe Christians, would they say we are openhanded and generous? Or would they talk about all the stuff we say we *don't* do?

I like the word "openhanded" in this verse. I think it's the opposite of tightfisted. I picture someone offering an open hand to provide help and support rather than extending a closed fist and dropping a few coins in a bucket. The difference between the two is what Dr. Wess Stafford, the president of Compassion International, is talking about when he describes his philosophy of caring for others. Dr. Stafford asks: When you serve the poor, do you see yourself bending down or sitting down? Do you see yourself sitting down *with* someone, or bending down *to* somebody? It's all about putting yourself on

an eye-to-eye level with someone rather than viewing yourself as superior.

Dr. Stafford often takes big donors out to see
the work their support enables Compassion to do. He
always tells these donors not to act as if the people
aided by these projects owe them anything—as if
the donors have done them a big favor. He reminds
his guests that in the kingdom of heaven, those who
have less are of a higher position. Jesus came to fulfill
the law and the prophets and to save the world, but
he also came to turn our social classes upside down.

LISTEN FIRST

If we want to offer help to those in poverty, we can't
just assume we have all the answers. Rather than
being so quick to offer advice, we need to begin by
listening. We should ask people what they need and
how we can help, rather than simply doing what we
think is best.

My little brother often quotes Proverbs 19:17:
"He who is kind to the poor lends to the Lord, and
he will reward him for what he has done." This verse
could be misinterpreted as, "If you are kind to the
poor, you're basically giving to God—so God will give
you lots of 'bling.'" I don't think that's how it works.
I think that when you help the poor, it brings you
joy—which is better than anything money can buy.
You also can find purpose in life through such service,
simply by using your gifts, skills, and talents to offer
an open, helping hand to those who need assistance.

Here's something to show how much God values giving to the poor. If you read the Bible, you may know Sodom was a city so evil that God destroyed it. What could have made an entire city so evil that God would actually torch the whole place? Were they all serial killers or something? What was the main problem with Sodom? A lot of Christians think it had something to do with sexual sin. But Ezekiel 16:49 tells us: "Now this was the sin of… Sodom: She and her daughters were arrogant, overfed and unconcerned; they did not help the poor and needy." Apparently, taking care of the poor and needy is a pretty big deal to God.

Recently, I was talking with some friends and I asked if they thought money was the answer to all the world's problems. They all said "no." But

> **About half the world's population lives on less than $2 a day per person.**
> (United Nations)

my mom was sitting there, and she said, "Maybe just throwing money at all the problems won't help, but a transfer of wealth would help many of them." I think she's right.

Most of us have so much. Pocket change to us might mean food for a month for someone else. Perhaps we could think about consuming less and giving more.

CHANGE IT: HEIFER INTERNATIONAL

Does your youth group go to summer camp each year? Well, what if, instead of attending your favorite beach or mountain camp, your group decided to spend a week living as if you were impoverished? That's what some students do through Heifer Global Passport Camp in Arkansas. Half the students in a group from First Presbyterian Church in Greer, South Carolina, spent a recent week living as though they were the poorest of the poor in the Mississippi Delta. Other young people from the group had a simulated experience of living in Tibet in huts.

The beauty of the Global Passport Camp is that it gives students a taste of the challenges the poor face every day. For many of them, it's an experience that deepens and sustains a commitment to working for lasting change. After attending the camp, youth groups are encouraged to get involved with Heifer International and meet some of the tangible needs others have.

Heifer International seeks to end poverty by providing a sustainable source of food and income to people living in poverty. Its first projects involved giving cows to people in small villages (hence the name Heifer International). A cow given to one family can actually help the whole village—the family can sell surplus milk, and a good cow will usually have one calf each year, which is then given to another family in the village. In a matter of years every family in the village has its own cow. Now Heifer has expanded to provide many different kinds of animals and care packages to people everywhere.

CHANGE IT: YOUR TURN

There are several ways you and your youth group can partner with Heifer International. I've learned of youth groups who have provided hives of bees, a goat, silkworms, a herd of sheep, and many other gifts that are really investments in a new life. You might have a bake sale and offer animal-shaped cookies to raise money to provide a needy family with an animal. Another idea is to "build an ark": Make a cardboard ark with paper cutouts of different animal pairs people can "buy" and add to the ark. When the ark is full, you've raised enough money to buy a farm animal for a family through Heifer International. (This would be a great project for younger kids, too.) You can learn more at www.heifer.org.

BRAINSTORM FOR CHANGE

- Two Dollars a Day: It's estimated that half the world's population lives on less than $2 a day. Try to live for a week on only $2 a day. Consider things like how much it costs to shower, how much your meals cost at home, and how much a pencil costs. It's basically impossible to live this way even for a week without skipping meals or asking other people for food. It seems crazy, but for many people around the world a dollar is a fairly hefty amount to live on a day. This project will deepen your solidarity with people who live this way, and maybe it will change the way you view your own wealth. Encourage your entire youth group to try this and then give the money you would have spent that week to an organization helping the poor.

- Microloans: Your group's donation to Heifer (www.heifer.org), Kiva (www.kiva.org), or Opportunity International (www,opportunity. org) could provide the seed money to help someone living in poverty begin a new life.

- Sponsor a child: Visit www.compassion.com and sponsor a child. Your investment over the long term will help break the cycle of poverty and give hope to a child for a lifetime.

- Rethink Christmas and birthdays: How much more do you really need? Check out www.adventconspiracy.org and see how you can spend less and give more. This may help you reclaim the joy of these celebrations. I learned about a little girl who asked people to put the money they'd have spent on a gift for her in

an envelope and then she donated
it all to help children in Africa.

It's amazing what five com-mitted guys can do. These friends founded an organi-zation called Dry Tears to bring clean and safe water to people in Africa and are inspiring others to do the same.

CHAPTER 6

HEALTH

*"He who has health, has hope.
And he who has hope, has everything."*

Ancient proverb

In a village in the Middle East, there were rumors of a great healer whose powers came directly from God. One day this healer was talking with teachers, religious leaders, and also anyone else who could come and listen. There were so many people the building was literally overflowing. Now, there were four guys in this town who had heard all about the wonderful things this healer could do. They had a friend they cared about very much who was paralyzed. Believing God's power was on this healer, they decided to try to get their friend in to see him. So each of them grabbed a corner of their friend's cot, and headed over to where the healer was. When they got there, they couldn't find a way in because of all the people.

These friends were very determined. Maybe they felt this was their friend's last chance to be well. They were willing to take drastic measures. One guy suggested they *climb up on the roof* and find a way to lower their friend down through the roof and into the room where the great teacher was. I don't know how they made it to the roof with their friend in tow, but they did. They then worked as a team to lower their friend down using ropes tied to the cot. When the healer saw the amazing faith they had, he said to the paralyzed man, "Friend, your sins are forgiven."

Now, this made a lot of the religious teachers angry. "Who is this fellow?" they thought to themselves. "Who can forgive sins but God alone?"

But the healer knew what they were thinking and said, "Why are you thinking these things? Which is easier: to say, 'Your sins are forgiven,' or to say, 'Get up and walk'?" So to let them know he had the power to forgive sins he said to the paralytic, "I tell you...*get up, take your mat, and go home.*" And he did.

Does this story sound familiar? I switched a few details, but you probably got by the end that the great healer was Jesus. The story's from Luke 5:17-26, and I'd really recommend going and reading it. But what's most important is that you understand the heart and meaning of this story. First of all, it's important to realize this is a historical event—*it really happened!* Jesus actually healed this guy because of the faith of his friends. Now think about that with me for a moment: These four friends climbed on top of a roof to lower their friend down to Jesus. These guys not only believed in God's healing power but also went the extra mile for their friend. They weren't afraid of looking foolish; they didn't stop trying to help their friend when the barriers looked too big; and they didn't try to talk one another into giving up because they were too tired and their friend's case too hopeless.

You can't escape news about serious health crises around the world. More than 42 million people are living with HIV/AIDS, and 74 percent of those infected people live in sub-Saharan Africa. Around the world, millions of children die each year from preventable diseases. Affordable health care is little more than a dream for many families. There are so many different kinds of cancer that it's mind boggling. It can be overwhelming to think about all these problems.

Like the four men who brought their friend to Jesus, I believe God wants us to have a part in healing the sick. I believe he wants us to be dedicated friends who relentlessly pursue health for our neighbors around the world. It may not happen in such a miraculous way, but God can use many methods to bring about healing—and you, your resources, and your influence might be among them.

CHANGE IT: DRY TEARS = CLEAN WATER

Conner Cress was a freshman in high school when he read an article about poverty in *World Vision* magazine. He learned that more than 1.1 billion people around the world don't have access to clean water. Many people have access only to water that is unhealthy, or that is so far away that those who go to fetch it (normally women and children) are in danger of exploitation. He read about children who are so dehydrated that they have no tears to cry; so they cry dry tears. Conner recalls staring in shock at these pages for what must have been an hour: "I felt like God was pointing at me saying, 'Look how blessed you are, Conner; just look around you and see how much I have blessed you with…now what are you going to do about that?'"

Conner realized he couldn't just ignore this problem—he knew he had to do *something*. He remembers pleading with God, asking God to give him an idea for responding to the problem of people who don't have enough water. Conner's solution started with a small idea of selling bracelets to raise money to dig wells and raise awareness. Conner told four of his closest friends—Dan Mirolli, Jared Ciervo, Logan Weber, and Kyle Blakely—about what he had read, and they decided to pool their money to buy 1,000 bracelets, and that's how Dry Tears

> **"I felt like God was pointing at me saying, 'Just look around you and see how much I have blessed you with… now what are you going to do about that?'"**
>
> Conner Cress

was started. By selling bracelets, water bottles, and T-shirts, Dry Tears raises money for clean water. But another great success of this student-led campaign has been the way the boys have raised awareness in their own church and high schools about the plight of people without clean water and how doable the solution really is.

Conner's parents say Conner was so impacted by the opportunity to do something bigger than himself that he uses every resource possible for the campaign. His mom, Teri, said, "Every time we would ask him about what he might want for Christmas, he would insist on nothing. He said he had plenty. If we wanted to give him something, we should give him money to go toward a well." Conner and some of the other guys have made a commitment to drink water most of the time as a way of reminding themselves of the needs of others.

Originally, Dry Tears supported the outreach efforts of Blood:Water Mission, but recently, Dry Tears has had opportunity to work directly with a village in Africa that needed clean, safe water. When Conner's dad went to Africa, the Dry Tears guys sent him with $1,000 dollars to meet a need if he encountered one. Dry Tears partnered with their church to build a well for a village that needed one. According to Conner's dad, Ted, "When a well goes into a village without clean water, the infant mortality rate there is cut in half. The people's chances of getting the typical illnesses associated with contaminated water are cut drastically as well. Statistics show that 80 percent of the diseases in Africa can be attributed to a lack of clean water. In this village, clean water will also mean church growth and community development." Another great thing about this well is that it's right next to a church, so the people who come to get water daily will also be exposed to the living water of Jesus Christ and can receive care for other needs they may have. The Dry Tears guys plan to stay in touch with the village to see what kind of difference the well makes.

Conner's parents say, "About a year before Dry Tears started, Conner told us he knew God had called him into the ministry. We all thought it was for his adult future. Little did we know that God would call him nine months later to start Dry Tears. We were very moved and in awe of our son's heart. We honestly had not realized just how deep his Christian worldview had grown. It did not surprise us that he had great compassion for the hurting, because he has always had that. It all made sense that he would put his heart of compassion into action. It caused us to worship God and give thanks for his loving hand on Conner's life."

Here's a way you can get involved: Make a commitment to drink only water for a week. (You can buy a water bottle from Dry Tears, or just use a bottle you have already.) Keep a record of every time you would have bought yourself a drink or grabbed one from the refrigerator, and set aside whatever money you would have spent. At the end of the week, send it in to Dry Tears. Even better, organize a group of your friends to do this. Not only will it help keep you honest, it'll raise even more funds that can help provide clean water for more people. Check out Dry Tears at www. drytears.org.

CHANGE IT: YOUR TURN

Nets for Nets: Preventing Malaria

It's estimated that an African child dies from malaria every 30 seconds. Malaria is a terrible illness that's spread through infected mosquitoes. There are affordable measures that can be taken to prevent the disease—but poverty makes even those solutions impossible for many people. One way to prevent the spread of the disease is through using chemically treated mosquito netting. The netting is

Measles, malaria, and diarrhea are three of the biggest killers of children—yet all are preventable or treatable.
(Care USA)

More than 30 million children in the world are not immunized against treatable or preventable diseases.
(Care USA)

500 million children have no access to sanitation.
(UNICEF)

400 million children do not have access to safe water.
(UNICEF)

270 million children have no access to health care services.
(UNICEF)

made of thin mesh that lets air in but keeps mosquitoes out. These nets are usually hung around beds to give each person a safe place to sleep.

I heard about a high school basketball team that decided to do something about the massive malaria epidemic. They decided to use their sport for good. For every three-point shot the team made, they would provide a mosquito net to a village where people are at risk of contracting the illness. This could also be done with a hockey team, soccer team, or any other team that uses nets. Your team could recruit sponsors to pledge support for the project. It's a creative way to use your sport to educate about a problem and help solve it.

Scavenger Hunt for Health-Care Items

Hope Ministries in Iowa has many great activities to help youth get involved in meeting the needs in their communities. One idea is a scavenger hunt for health-care items. Basically, it's a twist on the old game, but instead of collecting useless things, this game collects items that will help meet real needs. Students and youth leaders would be divided into small groups and would begin the hunt at the church or some designated meeting place——hopefully somewhere close to a lot of pharmacies or drugstores. The church could give each of the groups maybe $35 to start, and a list of health-care items to go buy. Each student might be asked to contribute $10 to join the party. A time limit would be set, and minimum quantities required for the items, so students have to be smart shoppers. For example, the list might say, "at least three tubes of toothpaste or four rolls of toilet paper." The amount of money the church provides should not cover all items on the list, so students know their money is actually going to help their neighbors as well. When everyone returns from the scavenger hunt, find the team who has the most items, and declare them the winners. (There probably shouldn't be a prize for winning—the prize is in having the chance to help others.) The youth group can then hand-deliver their items to the nearest co-op, homeless shelter, or other such organization.

BRAINSTORM FOR CHANGE

- Vitamin Drive: Have a vitamin drive where each student brings in a bottle of vitamins to provide to a free medical clinic or free food pantry.

- Band-Aid: Hold a concert and, as part of the admission fee, have people bring boxes of Band-Aids to give to medical missionaries and homeless shelters.

- Volunteer: Give your time to help clean, file, or do office work at a community-based free health clinic.

- Exercise class: Lead a free exercise class at a local community center to help people lead healthier lives.

- Coach: Offer to help coach a sports team in a poor community or offer a free sports clinic for kids who might not have opportunity to attend a sports camp.

- For more ideas, check out these other great organizations doing work on health-related issues: Mercy Ships, Children's Hospitals, Make-A-Wish Foundation, and World Vision.

Through books of Hope,
North American school
children write and illustrate
books to provide to children
around the world who oth-
erwise may not have access
to books of their own.

CHAPTER 7

EDUCATION

> *"In the boy there's a voice*
> *In the voice there's a calling*
> *In the call there's a promise*
> *And it won't quiet down"*
>
> Sara Groves, "In the Girl There's a Room"

EDUCATION: FOR THE PRIVILEGED FEW?

Most American kids view education not as a privilege but as a chore. It's not that we take it for granted—many of us actually hate going to school, and we talk about how much we hate it with our friends. Some students who do well in school play dumb because we think it isn't cool to be smart. Well, education is a privilege—as well as a right and a requirement for every child in the United States. *Sadly, it's not that way in many other parts of the world.*

Throughout the world many children have no expectation they will be provided with an education——free or otherwise. They don't expect to own a book or ever learn to read. Some experts believe illiteracy is the biggest contributing factor to poverty. A good education can break the cycle of poverty in a family. Teach a child math and he can get a good job. Teach a child to read and write and she may become a world-famous author. Educate children in history so they won't forget their heritage. With education, the possibilities are limitless.

Most people understand that knowledge is power. Knowledge gives you access to a better-paying job, to more opportunities, to people who have influence. But have you ever met someone who loves knowledge? You know, someone who reads a lot, researches a lot, loves to learn from the past in order to be better prepared for the future. People like that seem to approach education with a sense of wonder and anticipation—— excited to discover something they didn't know before. They also are really interesting to talk with.

My friends Alex and Brett Harris are like that. Alex and Brett are twins, and together they've launched an effort called "The Rebelution." Their goal is to motivate our generation to rebel against low expectations and to excel in all things. They believe our teen years should be a time to acquire knowledge and prepare ourselves for the future by taking on difficult challenges, pursuing wisdom, and seeking God. They've just written a book called *Do Hard Things*, and I'm really excited to read it and see what kind of encouragement they have to offer. I think one reason they've been able to accomplish so much is that they have prepared well by devouring books, listening to others, and being diligent students.

In the United States there's a lot of talk about giving every kid the opportunity to have an excellent education. But not every kid lives in a home where education is supported, and not every school has the necessary resources to provide all its students with the right training. These are things many of us take for granted.

EDUCATION AS A VACCINATION

In addition to promising a brighter future, education can help prevent many immediate problems. In many parts of the developing world, a child or adult who is illiterate is vulnerable to being oppressed or exploited. Oppressors want to keep people illiterate because it makes them easier to control. Modern-day slaves are often deceived and kept in captivity with false claims of debts owed. If slaves are taught to read and write, they are elevated from ignorance. They are more aware of their rights. They are given a renewed sense of self-worth.

Illiteracy can also make someone feel forced into crime because they are unable to find a job. Let's say there's a guy who lives in a big city and never

> *"Poverty and desperation can make someone feel trapped. Education can be the doorway that opens options for someone in a bad situation."*

learned to read. Suppose he has a wife and two kids—how is he going to support them? Who wants to hire a guy who can't read? He may be qualified to do all kinds of work, but he's unable to read the want ads or surf the Internet looking for job opportunities. Think about how desperate this person might feel. Maybe he'll resort to crime so he has money to feed his family—feeling there's no other way. I'm not saying he'd be right to commit such a crime. I'm just saying poverty and desperation can make someone feel trapped. Education can be the doorway that opens options for someone in a bad situation.

Throughout history we've seen examples of how education can propel someone to greatness. In my own family I've witnessed what it means for someone to be born in poverty and strive for a good education, get a scholarship to attend a college he could never have afforded, and then go on to provide a better life for himself and his children. One of my heroes is Frederick Douglass, a man who won his own freedom from slavery and then went on to become an educated man, an eloquent speaker, and an author. He was well read and this helped him gain the credibility to spread his message and bring freedom to others.

My friend Given Kachepa, whom I wrote about in my last book, is a modern-day Frederick Douglass who has taught me about the value of education. Given came to America from Zambia when he was a young boy to sing in a boys choir. It was hard for him to leave his family and everything familiar to him, but he was motivated by the promise he'd receive a good education. The people sponsoring the choir also said they'd provide a school and education for Given's siblings and friends. Unfortunately, that promise was a lie that was used to enslave Given and other boys. Through a series of events, Given was freed and now lives with a family in Texas who give him the love and care he deserves. He concentrates on his studies and has made his education a huge priority. He's turned down incredible speaking opportunities because he doesn't want his education to suffer. Given works hard and tries to take advantage of every opportunity to get the education he once could only dream about. While many others in our generation complain about the demands of their school workload, Given sees his education as a gift.

CHANGE IT: MICHELLE'S STORY

I recently had the chance to hear a young woman named Michelle Tolentino speak. She's very petite but packs a powerful message. Michelle was born in one of the most congested areas in Manila in the Philippines. She said it was basically the slums. Michelle was one of 17 people living in her one small house. Both her parents were unemployed, and there were lots of drug and alcohol problems in her community. She said it was common to see men drinking outside while their wives gambled and their little children ran up and down the streets outside, naked. Many of these parents seemed to have little hope for their children's future. Like many men in her neighborhood, Michelle's father was a drug abuser. When she was a little girl, fighting erupted in her home when other members of the household accused her father of stealing from them. Her father left, and from then on, she was a fatherless child. Michelle said her relatives hated her because she looked like her father. "They would tell me, 'You are so ugly. You will grow up like your father because you look like him.'" Imagine hearing those words from the people in your life who were supposed to care for you. Michelle said she felt "worthless, and that I am nothing, and that I have no future."

Eighteen percent of the world's population is illiterate.
(Unesco)

More than 60 percent of all inmates in U.S. prisons are functionally illiterate.
(Unesco)

Eighty-five percent of all juveniles who interface with the U.S. juvenile court system are functionally illiterate.
(Unesco)

Hope glimmered in Michelle's life when she became a part of a Compassion International project near her home. She discovered that Jesus loves her, and received her first Bible—a gift that was very precious to her. In her new Bible she read that God is "a father for the fatherless children like me." The family who sponsored her through

Compassion demonstrated God's love for her. "They would say in their letters, 'Our dear Michelle, you are so beautiful and precious to us, and we are so proud of you. We are praying for you; we love you.'" God used her sponsors to build up Michelle's broken-down self-image and give her hope.

Compassion also gave Michelle a chance to pursue her dreams by getting an education—something that wouldn't have been possible otherwise. She is now the youngest marketing head of a theater company in Asia. And she's taking the hope she's been given and passing it along. Michelle now sponsors a Compassion child of her own—a little boy named Andrew. She says she wants Andrew to "know that Jesus Christ loves him." After asking God to restore her relationship with her father, Michelle was able to forgive him, and now her family has been restored. Compassion inspired Michelle to greatness, and she is truly great.

I was really moved by Michelle's story. First, I was struck by how many of the things I take for granted (a caring family, a good education, and support from others) just isn't a reality for many. I was also amazed by the great potential within that little girl who was living in the slums of Manila—potential that might have gone unrealized without an education and the love shown by her sponsor family.

One of the things I most appreciate about Compassion International is the all-encompassing approach they have to child sponsorship. I've heard several other young adults speak who benefited as children from being sponsored by a family through Compassion International. They almost always talk about how incredible it was to get the chance to receive an education. You can be a part of making those dreams come true for even more children!

CHANGE IT: YOUR TURN

Books of Hope Project

Students in the United States—often elementary school students—are involved in helping boost literacy around the world. In some parts of the world, children who live in deep poverty or have been rescued from slavery and oppression are learning to read and speak English as part of their training for a more promising future. But often these kids cannot afford the books needed to build a library. Enter American children and the Books of Hope project. U.S. students visit the Books of Hope Web site, choose a topic to research, and then write and illustrate a book for a child in another part of the world. This program develops better reading and writing skills of students in U.S. schools and puts the American children in contact with the suffering around the world they might not know about otherwise. But the core focus of Books of Hope is about the children on the receiving end of these books. Not only do these kids have a chance to learn a new language, but the books can provide inspiration and even therapy for children who have been abused or neglected.

Individual U.S. schools can sponsor other schools around the world, sending books made by students as well as other school supplies. Right now, Books of Hope works with schoolchildren in Uganda and India. Kelsie, a North American elementary school student who participated in Books of Hope said, "Doing the children's book assignment was cool. I liked it because it was fun to be creative and write for a child's mind. It was inspiring to know that I might bring happiness to a child in Uganda and India.".

BRAINSTORM FOR CHANGE

- Sponsor a child through Compassion International at www.compassion.com.

- Volunteer as an after-school tutor at a community center or Boys & Girls Club.

- Spend an afternoon a week at a local library doing live readings to preschool children.

- Conduct a book drive at your school, providing books for children who can't afford their own.

Shauna, founder of A Million Thanks, reads through one of the millions of letters that have been written to express thanks to members of the Armed Forces.

CHAPTER 8

THANKS

> *"I would maintain that thanks are the highest form of thought, and that gratitude is happiness doubled by wonder."*
>
> Gilbert K. Chesterton

Many say our generation is materialistic and self-centered. They also say kids today are ungrateful. These are serious problems, but I don't think they're unique to our generation. I see materialism all around me. I see people of all ages who don't appreciate all the good things they have. I see people who seem to feel they are entitled to the service and sacrifices of others and don't seem to think those others are deserving of even a simple "thank you." I've observed a lack of thankfulness among both young folks and old—including myself.

I think the root of this is a whacked-out perspective. If we truly believed everything we have and all we receive (including acts of kindness) are gifts from a generous God, then we'd be more thankful. If we didn't think we'd earned everything based upon our own strengths, merits, and good looks, then we'd be more thankful. If we didn't take someone serving us as a sign of our own success and power, then we'd be more thankful.

> **"If we didn't take someone serving us as a sign of our own success and power, then we'd be more thankful."**

We take so many things for granted. When you pray (if you pray), do you thank God you have a warm bed to sleep in on a cold winter's night? Do you thank God for your friends and your family? Many of us offer a quick prayer of thanks when we sit down to eat, but do we really think about *why* we should be thankful? Why should we? Most of us eat all the time, or at least we have the opportunity. Did your parents ever say, "You need to finish your _____ (really disgusting food), there are starving children in Africa who would love to eat what you won't." Isn't that annoying? That's almost like forced thankfulness—someone trying to guilt you into eating your food and being thankful. But it's true that one of the reasons we should be thankful for food is because so many people don't have enough to eat. One reason we should be thankful for clothes is that so many people don't have them.

We have so many things to be thankful for. Chances are, if you went out and bought this book (or even if someone gave it to you), you probably have food to eat every day and a roof to sleep under at night. Don't take these things for granted.

Often, we don't even thank people for doing their job well. People who serve others every day in restaurants, tire shops, hotels, and other places rarely get thanked. For some reason, people who work in "service" industries hardly ever get thanked by those they serve! Why is that? The people who work in the drive-thrus have feelings, too! Why do we disrespect those who serve us?

Even our parents! How often do we thank the people who brought us into this world? If your mom packs your lunch, thank her, and tell her you love her. If your dad gets off work early to pick you up from school, thank him. Thankfulness is a step in the right direction for serving others.

CHANGE IT: SHAUNA AND A MILLION THANKS

When Shauna Fleming was 15, she was concerned that the many people serving in the U.S. military were not told often enough that Americans are thankful for their sacrifice. She didn't have family or friends serving in the military, but still felt compelled to do something. "I wanted to make sure our troops still felt appreciated and supported," she explains. "I decided writing letters of appreciation would be the best way of relaying this message."

It's been four years since Shauna launched the A Million Thanks Campaign. Because of her efforts, more than 2.6 million letters and emails have been sent to men and women serving in the military. Shauna says there are times when the campaign has been really demanding. What keeps her going are the emails she gets from soldiers who tell her how much the letters mean to them. "It's a great feeling," she says.

Shauna says she's learned a whole lot during the campaign. But more than anything, she's learned not to take things for granted—to be more thankful.

She's starting a new foundation called Wounded Soldiers Wish to raise money to grant the wishes of injured soldiers. You can learn more about (and get involved with) Wounded Soldiers Wish or A Million Thanks at www.amillionthanks.org.

CHANGE IT: YOUR TURN

Think about what a difference it might make if every kid in your school wrote just one thank-you note a week to someone who serves or cares for them. Think about the difference that might make for all the teachers, principals, janitors, assistants, grandparents, parents, pastors, policemen, soldiers, and other people who rarely get thanked.

You may not be able to solve world hunger immediately, but you can build someone up today just by thanking him or her. Take the time to thank the people around you, and take the time to thank God for all he has done for you. Practicing thankfulness is something we can do in our day-to-day lives to make this world a better place.

BRAINSTORM FOR CHANGE

- Start a Thanksgiving Journal in which you write down things—big and small—that happen each day that you're thankful for. Also, jot down Bible verses, poems, and song lyrics about being thankful.

- Keep small gifts like a roll of Lifesavers, a pack of gum, or sticky notes you can give to people just to let them know you're thankful for them.

- Make a commitment to always thank people who serve you at a restaurant or drive-thru. Think about adding "Thanks, I appreciate that." "Thanks, I hope you have a great day." "Thanks, this looks really good."

- Get a roll of gold stars and give them out to people who do nice things as a way of acknowledging them and saying thanks. It might sound cheesy—but what a fun, throwback way to acknowledge someone doing good.

- On your birthday, send a small gift and a card of thanks to your parents, your pastor, teachers, and others who have invested in your life.

- Always tip for good service. Consider writing a note on the bill with the server's name on it, saying, "Thanks, you did a great job tonight. We enjoyed our meal. God bless you."

River Community Church held a Style Your Soul event where students designed and painted on their own white Tom's Shoes. For each pair of shoes they purchased, a child would receive a pair of shoes he or she normally couldn't afford. Students got some really cool shoes while also doing good!

CHAPTER 9

CLOTHING

> *"I tell you the truth, whatever you did for one of the least of these brothers of mine, you did for me."*
>
> Jesus, Matthew 25:40

In our culture the clothes we wear say a lot about us. People invest a lot of time, effort, and money on clothing. We want to look good, and we judge other people based on how they dress. People sometimes assume that if a guy is wearing this kind of jacket or those shoes, then he must be that kind of person. Or someone might say, "I need to ask her where she got that!" (This is hypothetical, guys, just bear with me!) How many decisions do we make about people because of how they look, even before we meet them?

A Bible teacher of mine once told me about a time when an elderly woman at the church was upset because a young man came into church wearing a baseball cap. She was outraged—and probably made a judgment about the kind of person he was. My teacher reminded us that we as Christians *are* the church, so it's actually more accurate to say he was wearing a hat *on* the church rather than *in* the church. But either way, because of the woman's judgment, the young man left the church and didn't come back.

If I'm being completely honest with myself, I have to say that I sometimes make judgments about people based on what they wear or how they look. I know there are some people who never have anything nice to wear. You know how it feels to get a new shirt or pants. And the confidence you feel from knowing you look good? Imagine never having that feeling. Not only that, but imagine that the clothes you do wear don't even protect you from the wind, rain, cold, or sun.

What if you only had one pair of shoes, and they had massive holes in the bottom? Or what if, like millions of people, you didn't have any shoes at all? It would be really easy to cut your feet, and they'd be vulnerable to infection and disease. How can we care so much about whether we are wearing the latest style, when other people have nothing at all to wear? For many people in our world, it's not about choosing *which* pair of shoes to wear, it's about having *any* shoes to wear. It's not about whether to wear a collared shirt or a T-shirt, it's about having a shirt.

I'm not trying to make you feel guilty; but I think it's important to understand that clothing is much more than a fashion issue for many people. For someone in America, having a suit, even an old one, could mean the difference between getting the job or not. A clean shirt and jeans could build the self-confidence of a high schooler living in poverty. A new pair of shoes could literally mean an extended life for a child in Africa.

Jesus even talked about how when we clothe the poor it's as if we've done an act of kindness to him directly. We'll talk about that passage from Matthew 25 a bit more in the next chapter. I think being part of Generation Change requires that we rethink some of the things we take for granted, and how much and what we do with our money is one of them.

> *"For many people in our world, it's not about choosing which pair of shoes to wear, it's about having any shoes to wear."*

CHANGE IT: SOLES 4 SOULS

The mission of Soles 4 Souls is to impact as many lives as possible through the gift of shoes. This organization takes donations of gently used and new shoes and delivers them to people who don't have any. Soles 4 Souls dispatches shoes to 16 different countries around the world. You can support their work by donating your own shoes, hosting a shoe drive at your school or church, or volunteering your own time. Check out www.soles4souls.org.

CHANGE IT: YOUR TURN

"Undie Sunday"

This is a pretty cool idea (with a pretty funny name) that can involve every age group. For a homeless or very poor person, new underwear can be a luxury. Most thrift stores and clothing distribution centers don't have stacks of underwear. I guess used underwear is not something most people feel good about donating! Schools and churches around America have been uniting on Undie Sunday each March to solve this problem. Families are encouraged to purchase and donate new underwear that is distributed to people in need. Since 2006, more than 155,000 pieces of NEW underwear and diapers have been donated. Check out what else they're doing at www.dignityuwear.org.

Check out these organizations that help provide clothing and shoes:

TOMS Shoes
www.tomsshoes.com

Association of Gospel Rescue Missions
www.agrm.org

Salvation Army
www.salvationarmy.org

Dignity U Wear
www.dignityuwear.org

Buy One, Give One

Here's a very simple idea to discourage materialism. It goes like this: For every pair of shoes you buy, you give away a pair of shoes; for every pair of pants you buy, you give away a pair of pants, and so on. Instead of accumulating more and more stuff, you think purposefully about what you buy, and give things away instead of hoarding. The practice encourages us to buy less and give more, helping us be more grateful for what we have and more conscious of materialism.

BRAINSTORM FOR CHANGE

- Take the extra buttons that come with your shirts and assemble sewing kits to help people in other countries mend their own clothing, and get paid to mend clothes for others. Send these to Extreme Response or a shelter in your area. (For more on Extreme Response, see the chapter on Friendship.)

- Make baby blankets out of fleece. You can find lots of patterns for fleece-fringed blankets online. My brother's class did this when he was in first grade—it's really easy. His class donated their blankets to a crisis pregnancy center.

- Have a Toasty Fingers and Toes drive and collect gloves and socks. Then take them to the homeless shelter and give them away yourselves.

- Many cities do a "Blanket the City" week in which people drop off blankets at many different stores. The blankets are given to the homeless and people living in shelters.

- Go to a thrift store and buy up a bunch of coats in various kid sizes. They're usually priced really well so your money will go a long way. Then arrange with a school in an impoverished area to distribute the coats to kids who don't have adequate clothing.

- Custom T-shirts are printed for many races, fairs, and other community events. Often there are many shirts left over and no way to sell them. Contact the organizers to see if you can have them donated to a shelter or thrift store.

- For a couple more great clothing-related ideas, check out *Style Your Soul* in the Creativity chapter and *Princess Closet* in the Friendship chapter.

One-of-a-kind bowls painted
by teens are purchased by
diners at Empty Bowls events
and then taken home as
reminders of the millions of
people who will go hungry
today.

CHAPTER 10

HUNGER

"The war against hunger is truly mankind's war of liberation."

John F. Kennedy

Many people in the world are without food. It's a common necessity many of us take for granted or even whine about daily. As I mentioned earlier, I think we minimize the problem when we pretend eating every vegetable on our plate at dinner will really make an impact on global hunger. Are we expected to gorge ourselves at every mealtime, or choke down Aunt Mabel's broccoli tuna surprise? That, in and of itself, will not provide the food hungry people need.

It would be great if some of us were less picky about what we ate, and it's never good to waste food, but I don't think the way to end world hunger is for every American kid to clean his or her plate every night. No, in order for us to make a change, to *be* the change in this area, we must do something. In this section I'll give you some ideas, you can implement right where you are.

It's interesting to me that the Bible says we "[do] not live on bread alone, but on every word that comes from the mouth of the Lord" (Deuteronomy 8:3). Jesus even quoted this very verse to Satan when he was being tempted to turn the rocks into bread. But it's equally true that Jesus and the rest of the Bible had a great deal to say about the importance of giving food to those who need it, and providing for people's physical needs.

I have heard some people say we shouldn't talk so much about feeding the hungry, ending slavery, or helping the poor when a whole generation of people need to know about Jesus. They ask me, "Why aren't you concentrating on salvation?" Well, let me clear things up a bit—and please read this carefully. I don't believe freeing slaves and making a better world is a replacement for following God and leading a generation to Christ. I believe it is an extension of following God and leading others to Christ. In other words, I don't think we can separate our call to change the world from our call to share the truth about Jesus and his sacrifice for people. God calls us not to one or the other, but to both.

I get to speak to a lot of non-Christian audiences, and I think "ministering" to them should include presenting the gospel but it also has to include caring about the things that keep them from being all God dreams they can be. Look at what Jesus says in Matthew 25:31-45:

> When the Son of Man comes in his glory, and all the angels with him, he will sit on his throne in heavenly glory. All the nations will be gathered before him, and he will separate the people one from another as a shepherd separates the sheep from the goats. He will put the sheep on his right and the goats on his left.
>
> Then the King will say to those on his right, "Come, you who are blessed by my Father; take your inheritance, the kingdom prepared for you since the creation of the world. For I was hungry and you gave me something to eat, I was thirsty and you gave me something to drink, I was a stranger and you invited me in, I needed clothes and you clothed me, I was sick and you looked after me, I was in prison and you came to visit me."
>
> Then the righteous will answer him, "Lord, when did we see you hungry and feed you, or thirsty and give you something to drink? When did we see you a stranger and invite you in, or needing

clothes and clothe you? When did we see you sick or in prison and go to visit you?".

The King will reply, "I tell you the truth, whatever you did for one of the least of these brothers of mine, you did for me."

Then he will say to those on his left, "Depart from me, you who are cursed, into the eternal fire prepared for the devil and his angels. For I was hungry and you gave me nothing to eat, I was thirsty and you gave me nothing to drink, I was a stranger and you did not invite me in, I needed clothes and you did not clothe me, I was sick and in prison and you did not look after me."

They also will answer, "Lord, when did we see you hungry or thirsty or a stranger or needing clothes or sick or in prison, and did not help you?"

He will reply, "I tell you the truth, whatever you did not do for one of the least of these, you did not do for me."

I thought I knew this story, but I've been missing out on a deep truth. Get this: Jesus separates them based on how they responded to people in need, whether they offered help or not. He doesn't ask, "How many people did you convert?" or "How many times did you tell someone about God's love?" Jesus wants to know what they did for the poor! That makes it pretty obvious that serving the poor and oppressed is a big deal to God.

How then can any Christian say we should concentrate *only* on saving people from hell without providing relief for suffering here? Shouldn't we be doing what we can to help free them from both eternal hell *and* hellish conditions on earth? How can we minimize the suffering of the poor and pretend that physical freedom and spiritual freedom don't go hand in hand?

Think of it this way: What if you were working in a soup kitchen and a woman came in who was really hungry? Would you hand her a Bible and send her away? Or would you give her soup, bread, and water—and by doing so, demonstrate the love of Christ? By giving her the nourishment she wants and needs, you may also win the credibility to share the gospel with her in a meaningful way.

> *"If one of you says to him, 'Go, I wish you well; keep warm and well fed,' but does nothing about his physical needs, what good is it?"*
>
> James 2:16

Please take this insight to heart and make it part of the way you view ministry. When serving those Jesus called "the least of these," it should be as if we are serving Jesus himself. Our gratitude to God for freeing us (spiritually and perhaps even physically) should motivate us to care for others and show compassion to the hurting. When the end comes, will we be among those who really served Jesus or do we think telling others about him is enough? I pray that my generation will be known as a group of believers who really live out their faith—that we'd not only be "saved," but that we'd sacrifice our own comforts so others can live without so much pain.

Jesus was very practical. Take a look at the story in Mark 8:1-9. Jesus doesn't chastise the hungry people who have gathered to hear him speak. His disciples seem to want to send the crowds away to get something to eat—just as they'd suggested in a similar situation in Mark 6:30-44. But Jesus says, "No, they might all pass out from exhaustion on their way home." So he asks the disciples, "What food do you have?" All they have is seven loaves and a couple of fish. Jesus takes the meager offering, blesses it, and feeds the 4,000 people—and even has some left over to provide an additional

Check out these other organizations helping to feed the hungry around the world and in your community:

Compassion International
www.compassion.com

Food for the Hungry
www.fh.org

Salvation Army
www.salvationarmy.org

World Relief
www.wr.org

World Vision
www.worldvision.org

blessing out of the abundance. I think Jesus was setting an example here: When there's a need, don't just feel sorry for people and send them on their way. Instead, find a way to meet the need.

We see the same spirit in the model prayer Jesus taught his disciples: "Give us this day our daily bread . . ." Clearly, Jesus placed an emphasis on day-to-day provisions whether they are spiritual or physical.

It's true you can't feed a hungry child elsewhere simply by deciding not to eat the burger in front of you. But what if you and your youth group decided to fast for a day, or maybe to fast from a certain type of food for a year (let's set high goals)? Then you could take the money you would have spent on that food and give it to a charity.

We often try to protect ourselves from getting too close to the suffering of others. Doing a food drive where you collect cans of food to send them to someone "over there" is great, but I also think it's great to go "over there" and get to know people who are in need of hope, friendship, and a good meal. Here are a few creative ideas for providing food to the hungry.

CHANGE IT: RYAN AND THE EMPTY BOWLS

A group of teenagers from Manlius, New York, took a trip one summer to serve in a West Virginia community where poverty was a significant issue. The kids from St. Ann's Church in New York came from dramatically different backgrounds than their new friends in West Virginia. The St. Ann's kids were privileged in many ways and were not used to going without or even seeing poverty up close. Like many of us, those kids had been focused on what our culture calls success: making the sports team, getting high SAT scores, staying on top of the latest trends. But for their trip to West Virginia, they shed their iPods, computers, and cell phones (I know, just thinking about this makes some of you sweat!) and went to serve.

According to the youth minister at St. Ann's, Kristy Vossler, the trip was "a holy experience" that far exceeded her wildest expectations. As happens so often, showing compassion was contagious, and the teens came home wanting to do more. Ms. Vossler said, "After our mission trip I said to the kids, it's great that we had a week to "feel good" helping others, but the real testament will be what we can *continue* to do to make a difference! I believe God wants us to come back to our community and use our talents and gifts. Will we be willing to answer that call?"

The 70 teens in that youth group were eager to answer that call. They began exploring some causes their youth group might take up. One student, Ryan, read about the Empty Bowls idea—a campaign started by a high school art teacher a few years ago. He prepared a detailed presentation about it for Ms. Vossler and the youth group. The kids spontaneously applauded and decided to get on board with the effort.

For their Empty Bowls effort, about 50 students created ceramic bowls. Each student designed two different bowls, and then went to a local pottery store where they could mold, fire, and paint the bowls they'd designed. They then invited families from the church to a fundraising dinner. Each family paid for the dinner and selected a favorite bowl to take home. They were encouraged to put the bowl on the family dinner table, empty, as a way of remembering the families around the world who go hungry each night and as a reminder to pray for them and to be thankful. The St. Ann's students raised $2,200 at their dinner, which was donated to the rescue mission in Syracuse, New York.

Ryan and his friends have seen how incredible it can be to work with God to be Generation Change. If you'd like to learn more about Empty Bowls and different ways students from around the country have implemented the idea, you can go to www.emptybowls.net.

CHANGE IT: YOUR TURN
Burrito Project

The Burrito Project was founded to feed the homeless using rice and beans—two foods that are pretty inexpensive and expand significantly when cooked. The burrito is a perfect meal for someone who is mobile, since it's wrapped up, self-contained, and full of nutritious ingredients. The idea has caught on and you'll find the Burrito Project in cities throughout the United States.

Students involved with the Burrito Project construct hundreds of burritos, and then go out and eat with homeless people. What I love about this is that this project requires you to literally GO OUT. So often we stay at home in our comfortable little bubbles, and try to avoid rubbing up against the problems we must face sooner or later in our world. The Burrito Project invites us to "provide conversation, friendship, and a hot meal to those who are often shunned or ignored in our society."

Another thing I like about the Burrito Project is that they don't want it to be all about their idea. They encourage groups to do a PB&J project or a falafel project if they prefer—it's all in keeping with their motto "'cause Momma said share." The project's Web site offers advice about navigating local laws about feeding the homeless as well as step-by-step instructions for building a quality burrito. Check it out at www.burrito-project.org or on their MySpace page.

852 million people in the world are hungry.
(Bread for the World Institute)

56 percent of the people who request emergency food assistance in the United States are employed.
(U.S. Council of Mayors)

Eleven million children younger than five die every year, more than half from hunger-related causes. 153 million children under five in the developing world are underweight.
(Bread for the World Institute)

Soup and Socks
The Soup and Socks page on MySpace

says, "We're a broke, non-profit, grassroots organization staggering on half a limb." But this group provides a simple concept that's easily implemented, doesn't require a lot of cash, and is entirely student-led (not unlike one of my favorite loose-change-raising abolitionist campaigns). Soup and Socks is an Atlanta-based group that tries to provide soup, socks, and conversation to the homeless in that city. The students get together weekly, make big pots of soup, round up the socks and other necessities that have been donated during the week, and head to a park where the homeless hang out. They invest their time talking with the people they're serving, getting to know their stories, and showing them that someone values and cares about them.

By the way, at the time I was completing this book, Soup and Socks needed just $750 more to become a certified 501(c)3. So if you want to go to their MySpace page and donate, that would be great. They also need assistance making a documentary; so let them know if you have skills in that area.

BRAINSTORM FOR CHANGE

- Sell food to buy food. Have a bake sale or a lunch where you really are selling food to buy canned goods and other necessities that can be donated to a local food bank or shelter.

- Pick a Country, Any Country: Choose a country and have a dinner featuring native dishes from that nation. Be sure to serve accurate portions so kids can relate to how much most people in that country would eat at a meal. Send all the proceeds to a nonprofit.

- Find out what items your local food bank needs most. Then go to a grocery store and ask the manager if the store would consider matching your donation of those items.

- Volunteer to help stock the food bank.

- Serve a meal at the local kitchen. This is especially helpful during the winter when workers are in short supply and the need to get out of the weather is greater.

- Go to your local bakery, bread store, or grocery store and ask what they do with their soon-to-expire food items. See if you can pick them up and deliver them to the shelter.

- Trick or Treat So Others May Eat: Go door to door on Halloween but instead of collecting candy, collect canned goods for your food shelter.

- Organize your church or school group to prepare brown paper bags packed with granola bars, nuts, dried fruit, water bottles, and other food items that don't spoil easily.

Encourage people to carry a bag in their car or backpack, so they have something available to offer a homeless or hungry person in need of assistance.

CHAPTER 11

TRUTH

> "Are you interested in revolution? Do you want to help solve the social ills of the world? We invite you to join with us in following the Greatest Revolutionary of the centuries. He is alive."
>
> Dr. Bill Bright

In the midst of a discussion on clean water, the health care crisis, poverty, and other social causes, delivering the truth about Jesus may seem like an old-fashioned idea. I'm afraid that may be truer than we'd all like to admit. I've spent a lot of my time the past four years speaking about supporting human rights and ending oppression and slavery. When I've spoken to audiences at Christian gatherings, I've assumed people understand that my work on these issues is an extension of my faith in Jesus. But now I'm starting to wonder about that.

More recently, I've gotten concerned this whole "activism thing" is in danger of becoming a new gimmick—especially in youth ministry. Working on social issues is the hip, new, cool thing to do. And I think it's awesome that so many young people are working to make the world a better place. But I worry that social projects have become the "thing" rather than an extension of The Main Thing—our faith in and love for Jesus.

I have a lot of friends who are youth pastors, and I'm told that when they get together they often talk about how many kids are involved in their groups. How many come on Sunday nights? How about Wednesdays? What kind of growth are you experiencing? There's a lot of pressure to get the numbers up.

A few years ago you'd have found most youth groups advertising their gatherings like this: Loud music! Fun Games! Hilarious Skits! Food!

Those things are all fine and good and fun. I LOVE music (and food...food is good.) These things may draw students in, but I think we've seen they don't change lives and build a growing, maturing group of teenage Jesus-followers.

Sometimes I worry that social projects get used the same way. Ask some youth pastors what their kids are learning about God and how God is working among them, and they may respond, "Well, we took a trip to build a house in Jamaica this spring...Oh, and there's that Burmese refugee thing we've been doing, and..."

"No, I meant what has God been teaching your kids...through his Word. The things that are personal and heart-changing truths."

"Uhhh...well we took this trip to Jamaica last spring and..."

Now, I do think that working for social justice and getting involved in the lives of the poor and oppressed has the potential to change lives. I've become a different person as I've worked to help end modern-day slavery. But at the heart of it all has been the way these experiences have deepened my relationship with Christ and brought me closer to the world God loves.

> *"Service shouldn't take the place of helping students learn about God and develop a deeper relationship with him. Instead, our service should be an extension of our faith."*

It seems like it should go without saying, but I'm pleading with you: If you're a youth worker, do not allow justice for the poor or acts of service to replace introducing your students to God, and helping them understand the deep truths written in his book, the Bible.

Service shouldn't take the place of helping students learn about God and develop a deeper relationship with him. Instead, our service should be an extension of our faith. My generation, my WORLD, is dying in the wilderness without God. Mission trips and service activities, in and of themselves, will not save us. It is God who saves.

So, while you're serving the poor, rescuing the oppressed, defending the orphan, and pleading for the widow, don't forget to keep the Word of God central to all you do. Study so you know what you believe and why. From that study will come a desire to know God better, and I believe that can be accomplished in part by serving others, whom he loves. As you sacrifice for others and seek to walk in the ways of Jesus, your service will have greater meaning and you will encounter God at deeper levels.

Those of us who know Jesus and are learning to follow him hold a precious treasure—one Jesus commanded us to share with others. Instead of keeping this

Check out these organizations that help deliver Bibles and equip you to share your faith:

Student Life
www.studentlife.org

American Bible Society
www.Bibles.org

The Navigators
www.navigators.org

Alpha International
www.alphainternational.org

Youth Specialties
www.youthspecialties.com

Young Life
www.younglife.org

treasure to ourselves, let's give it away liberally. Let's help one another and new believers understand and live out the deep truths found in the Bible. It would be a tragedy to keep this treasure hidden for ourselves, instead of sharing with the hurting people we care for in Jesus' name.

CHANGE IT: DARE2SHARE

Dare2Share is a group that equips young people to share their faith and change the world. I heard about a Dare2Share speaker who was talking to a large gathering of students, encouraging them to tell their friends about their faith in Jesus. He was encouraging them to study the Bible and to be deliberate about sharing their faith. He pulled out his cell phone and had everyone else do the same. Then he had everyone make a call on the spot to a friend that's not a Christian and tell them about Jesus. All the kids were panicking, but the pastor really was calling a friend. One by one, the kids began to each call a friend and tell him or her about Jesus Christ. You can learn more about Dare2Share and get equipped at www.dare2share.org.

CHANGE IT: YOUR TURN

Used Bible Drive

Many American Christians have several Bibles sitting around their home that they rarely use, because those Bibles have been replaced with newer ones or preferred translations. Consider a Bible drive where people can bring Bibles they are no longer using. The Bibles can then be donated to a homeless shelter, Salvation Army, a missionary, or someone else who could distribute free Bibles.

Feast on the Word

When your church has a potluck, picnic, or some other gathering, have everyone bring along a new Bible to donate to your missions teams to distribute.

Loaded iPods

Our church purchased a bunch of iPods and loaded them with an audio version of the Bible, sermons from trusted pastors, and other audio books and resources that teach about the Bible or help people grow spiritually. The iPods were given to members of the church serving on short-term missions to distribute. Often, the iPods are given to people serving as pastors who have little formal training.

Get Equipped

Start a small group that studies the basics of the faith. There are all kinds of terrific Bible studies available you can do together. Rather than choosing something topical, choose a study that focuses on the foundation of your faith.

BRAINSTORM FOR CHANGE

- Each week choose a new verse to memorize and post it on your mirror, in your car, etc. It's like planting a seed into the soil of your heart, a seed that will grow and serve you through your whole life.

- Gather some mature Christian friends and role-play a conversation in which you'd answer questions and concerns about faith your friends who don't yet know God might have.

- Read a book about or by a great teacher, preacher, or missionary from the past. Some of my favorites are Jonathan Edwards, George Müller, C. S. Lewis, Jim Elliot, Corrie ten Boom, and Dr. Martin Luther King Jr.

- Volunteer to teach or disciple younger children through your church's Sunday school, Young Life's Campaigners or WyldLife program, or another group.

Students at Providence Christian Academy outside Atlanta spend a day cleaning up common spaces in their community.

CHAPTER 12

ENVIRONMENT

> *"Earth provides enough to satisfy every man's need, but not every man's greed."*
>
> Mahatma Gandhi

There's a lot of controversy surrounding global warming and saving the environment. But even *if* all of what is said about global warming and other environmental concerns is not true, there is one thing that is clear: People of faith are obligated to take care of God's earth.

I think it's unfortunate that activism related to environmental or human-rights issues is often considered to be a "liberal thing." Instead, I think we should make caring for people and the planet a "Christian thing"—something followers of Jesus are known for and expected to do.

In his book *Saving God's Green Earth*, Tri Robinson talks about feeling very nervous when he began to speak out about how we were misusing the environment. He knew he would take some heat on the issue. But God had placed it on his heart, and he could not remain silent. Tri says, "All of God's creation is important to him, down to the last sparrow and blade of grass. One of God's first commands to mankind was to 'tend his garden.'" I believe you can see God's work in all aspects of his creation—in people, in plants, and in animals.

> **"God saw all that he had made, and it was very good..."**
>
> Genesis 1:31

God told Adam and Eve they had authority over all creation. Some people think that means we are free to do whatever we want to this earth God has given to us. But think of it this way: Imagine a close friend has given you a massive plot of land on which they had lovingly planted a beautiful botanical garden and animal sanctuary. Your friend had planned carefully what it would take to sustain the plant and animal life and had planted and built accordingly. I would hope that you, as the receiver of the gift, would show your appreciation by taking care of the property, by doing your best to maintain the balance your friend had worked so hard to achieve that allows all the plants and animals to thrive. You might harvest the fruit on the trees, but you probably wouldn't thoughtlessly cut them down. You wouldn't knowingly introduce contaminants that would kill the fish and animals that lived there.

I think it's the same with this gift, this earth, on which God has placed us to live. He has provided all we need to sustain our lives—plants, animals, and the habitats to support their lives. Taking care of the earth is simply showing kindness and appreciation for God's goodness and all he's given us.

I've heard some people say, "Well, Jesus is coming back and he's gonna burn up the earth anyway, so we might as well just use it all up." I think that's sort of like viewing the world as a big vending machine, where we just take and take and never put anything back. We don't know when Jesus will return. Until that day, I think we should carefully steward and tend to the earth God has given us.

> **245.7 million tons of municipal solid waste were collected in the United States in 2005.** (EPA)

CHANGE IT: YOUR TURN

Students are doing all kinds of great things in their own communities and around the world to help the environment. Some of these ideas might seem simplistic compared with the many different "big" solutions people are discussing to address major environmental problems. But there are many things you can do to help the earth right away.

One way is to help your school develop a recycling program. Most high schools have drink machines, but many don't have recycling bins nearby—so students just trash the cans. Get permission to put recycling bins near the machines and have the cans recycled, then use the money to buy library books or other items the school needs.

BRAINSTORM FOR CHANGE

- Clean it up: I read about some students in Georgia who tackled an overgrown and littered area of their community with rakes, shovels, and mulch, and planted new trees and shrubs. This can be done anywhere. Another group of students studying ecology in California planted hundreds of trees along a city street that really needed some beautifying. Those trees will improve air quality, provide a safe haven for birds and other animals, and create some community pride. Learn more about that effort at www.pacoimabeautiful.org.

- Recycling for neighbors: A group of students at Mars Hill Bible Church in Michigan learned that some of their neighbors were unable to pay their heating bills during the cold Michigan winters. These resourceful students started a recycling project to turn cans into cash, and then used that money to help pay the heating bills of their neighbors. They were helping others and helping the earth at the same time.

- Memory garden: When my grandmother passed away, she didn't want a big funeral or fancy gravestone. Our family decided to plant a garden of roses (her favorite flower) at the high school in the small town where she grew up. This is a great way to pay tribute to someone and improve the environment at the same time. You could also do this as a birthday or anniversary gift, planting a tree or flowers in someone's honor.

High school art students participate in Project Memory, using their talents to provide orphans with beautiful portraits.

CHAPTER 13

CREATIVITY

> *"The foundation of our creativity is our Creator. Because we are made in the image of God, our creativity and faith are intertwined."*
>
> Alice Bass

*C*reativity might seem like a strange word that doesn't quite match the other titles. When I talk about "creativity" I mean things we can bring into the lives of others that may not be a matter of life or death, but that bring beauty and richness into people's lives and the world. I don't think God wants his children to simply survive; I think God wants us all to have lives that are rich and full and abundant. And I think creativity is one thing that enriches our lives and our world. Creativity moves people beyond mere survival and allows them to thrive.

I really enjoy art of almost every type. Painting, sculpture, photography, music, film—I appreciate all kinds of creativity. Did you know God places a high value on creativity and innovation? God is the source of all creativity, more creative than the best human artists. Creation shouts his artwork. Check out the book of Psalms—they show the poetry God can inspire in a person. I've never read anything else like them. I've written some poetry, and I've read lots of other poets, but no one I've seen has succeeded in copying the form and format of the Psalms.

When I was in Australia, I had the privilege of hearing a youth pastor named Paul Andrew speak. He was talking to a group of youth leaders about innovation and creativity. He was challenging us to think creatively—to reflect the character of God by embracing innovation and creativity. He wasn't encouraging people to just think up weird new ideas just for the sake of being different—it was deeper than that. I think he was challenging us to ask God for fresh ways to communicate and new ideas that help us see things from a different perspective.

Did you know that God only creates good things? If you look in the book of Genesis, God describes everything he created as good. The only thing he said was not good was the fact that Adam was alone, but he solved that problem right away. I like to think God filled the earth with such beauty and wonder not only to display his glory but also for our enjoyment. Why else would he give food such a rich variety of tastes? Why else would God fill our world with light and color and sound and scent? Why do the leaves change color instead of just falling from the trees? I believe God created those good things for our enjoyment.

I also believe that when the Bible says God made us in his image, this means he planted a bit of his own creative capacity and desire to create within us. I think that's why so many artists feel a spiritual connection through their art, and also why so many people seek to make the world a better place through their own artistic talents. I believe that when we express our own creativity, we imitate the One who created us all.

Switchfoot's Jon Foreman is one of my mentors who has helped me think about how art reflects the character of God and the problems of our hurting world. Recently Jon told me he thinks sometimes the artist's role is to provide a way of getting the pain out— of demonstrating the suffering in the world when simple words are not enough. Jon also reminded me that God hurts when he sees people suffering. We have a compassionate God who understands us. God knows beauty, but he also knows pain and loss. The artist creates works that demonstrate that to the world.

I've been blessed to have relationships with many artistic people, including people who make a living creating. To me, they are proof of God's creative character. And, they're evidence that beauty can exist in a broken world.

CHANGE IT: THE MEMORY PROJECT, BEN'S STORY

When Ben finished college, he didn't have a clue what he wanted to do for a career. "All I knew," Ben says, "was that, just like millions of other people who are dedicated to love and kindness, I wanted to help make the world a better place (assuming, of course, that any of us even know what a 'better' world would be)!"

Ben's desire to make a difference started him on a journey that led to a service project at an orphanage in Guatemala. "I had never worked with kids before, so my first sight of so many children in the company of so few adults was rather surreal," he recalls. "There was no health care worker at the orphanage, and since I had arrived with a bag full of donated medicine, it was somehow determined that I should serve as the orphanage "doctor." The highest medical training I had ever received was Red Cross first-aid training, so I was incredibly ill prepared for the job. I ended up leaving with a sunken head, feeling like I hadn't really done anything at all."

Ben came back home to the States, wishing he could just forget what he'd seen. He felt powerless to do anything to make a difference for those hurting kids. He spent part of a year traveling around and volunteering at various ministries, but never put down roots anywhere. One day he was thinking about a man he'd met at the orphanage in Guatemala. This man had told them that he too was an orphan, and that he didn't have any belongings to help him remember his childhood. Ben remembers, "We were all taking pictures in order to remember our experience there, and he suggested we develop copies of our pictures to share with the kids. It struck me very deeply that his advice did not have anything to do with the kids' 'basic needs,' but rather needs relating to their self-identity. His parting message was, 'You guys should help the kids hang on to special keepsakes that will aid them in developing a sense of who they are as unique individuals.'"

Imagine if, as you were growing up, no one ever took a picture of you. No photos from soccer games or birthdays or graduations. No yearbook photos, no vacation pictures—nothing to document your growing up. Would you feel unloved?

Ben began to think about the psychological and emotional consequences for kids who grow up in orphanages with little sense of identity or history. A gifted artist, Ben decided to begin painting portraits of children in orphanages that could be given to kids as a way to help them remember their childhoods and know that someone cares about them. In what is now known as the Memory Project, Ben has invited art teachers and advanced art students to join him in providing

> *"I believe my talents are a gift from God, and I am to use them to fulfill his purposes in my life and in his world."*
>
> Janice Elsheimer

portraits to orphans. When high school students participate in the Memory Project, they are assigned a child somewhere in the world who has been "abandoned, orphaned, abused, or neglected." Each student creates a custom portrait of his or her child. By the end of the 2007-2008 school year, 16,500 portraits will have been painted as part of the project.

Ben reflects, "Now, I certainly don't believe that simply handing a child a portrait of herself will make her life complete. But if that portrait captures the beauty within her, and if she is touched to know that someone far away spent hours making it for her, then that portrait just might brighten her life in its own small way. Our society needs people to create art, because art can remind us what life is all about and provide inspiration for the future." Learn how you can participate at www.thememoryproject.org.

CHANGE IT: YOUR TURN

Style Your Sole

TOMS Shoes is an innovative company founded by Blake Mycoskie that not only makes cool shoes but also provides shoes for poor children around the world. For every pair of shoes you buy from TOMS, they provide a pair for someone who cannot afford them. They recently completed a shoe drop in South Africa where thousands of kids were given a pair of shoes (for some their very first) to wear to protect their feet from injury and disease.

One great way to get involved with TOMS Shoes is to plan a Style Your Sole party. Each of the friends you invite to the party pays a fee in advance and gives you his or her shoe size. Before your party you'll receive a shipment with a pair of plain white TOMS Shoes for each guest. You provide paint, fabric, stencils, etc., and your friends all design and paint their own unique pair of TOMS. At the end of the night, each person not only has a great new one-of a-kind pair of shoes, but you all know that for every pair of shoes purchased for your event, another pair will be sent to a child somewhere in the world. Now that's what I call a party! For more info, check out www.tomsshoes.com.

BRAINSTORM FOR CHANGE

- Have your art class create pieces around a topic such as justice, poverty, or the environment and then hold a gallery exhibit and art auction to benefit the cause.

- Write and perform a drama or hold a poetry competition that brings to light the struggles of others around the world.

- Paint a mural in a community center.

- Volunteer to teach painting, dance, a craft, or some other talent at a Boys & Girls Club. Art programs have been cut from many schools.

Your time with these kids may be a key opportunity for them to explore their creativity and artistic talent.

- Support organizations that provide band instruments to kids who otherwise couldn't afford them.

- Volunteer to offer free music lessons in a low-income area of your community.

- Students at one church created oversized canvasses depicting their ideas about freedom that were then displayed in the foyer as a reminder of the need to seek justice.

- Wear your cause by purchasing one of Jedidiah's cool shirts. The Hope Collection by Jedidiah sportswear is a series of shirts designed to speak out about problems facing the world today. Jedidiah gives a portion of the profits to the nonprofits featured on the shirts. You can buy Jedidiah gear at www.jedidiahusa.com or at Buckle Stores.

- For more art- and creativity-based suggestions, check out *Empty Bowls* in the Hunger chapter.

I had the privilege of speaking to a group of youth leaders within the Korean United Methodist Church. At first I wondered why they would be interested in having a white kid like me speak to a group of all Korean students. Then I decided it would be a great opportunity to put myself in the shoes of others who are often the only person of their race at an event and it would be a great chance to get to know more about my brothers and sisters in Christ who are first- or second-generation Korean-Americans. It was a great experience!

CHAPTER 14

UNITY

> **"We must learn to live together as brothers or perish together as fools."**
>
> Dr. Martin Luther King Jr.

Sometimes unity can seem like a distant dream—or like a New Year's resolution that begins with great intentions only to fall apart when the going gets too hard.

Recently I was talking with some guys from my school about the spiritual retreats students from our school go on each year. The common message at each retreat is we need to create more unity among all the students. We all then come back home and settle in at lunch on Monday with our same old groups of friends—in the comfort zone. My friends and I were wondering why that always happens. Maybe it's because there's no plan. Or maybe there's no real desire to see change.

This lack of unity may not seem hurtful at first. It's not surprising we might choose to spend time with those who are most like us—or who like us—rather than reaching out to someone new or stretching ourselves. But if we only build relationships with the people who seem most similar to us, we miss out on an opportunity to build our character and prepare well for our future.

The things we say to and about other people can either build unity or destroy it. And building unity is about more than just the obvious things like not dissing people to their faces or gossiping about them behind their backs. You build unity by apologizing when people tell you that you've hurt them. You build it by being careful not to say something that might offend someone else, even if you don't see a problem with it. You don't say things just for the shock factor, since that can also destroy unity. I think we students often get a kick out of playing devil's advocate—choosing an opposite point of view just for the sake of an argument. But if we are always disagreeing, how can we ever hope to build true community?

One of the biggest barriers to unity is our own selfishness. We are all selfish—it's part of our sinful nature. People often fight because of selfish desires. Most arguments happen because someone doesn't get his or her way. It's always "about me"—and we easily get offended or angry when we don't get what we want. It all comes back to "me" and "I."

There is also a particular kind of division I wanted to talk about that is very harmful and shouldn't exist in God's family. It's been said for a while that the church is the most segregated place in America. In my own experience, this appears to be true—and to me it's very sad. As I've studied the abolition of slavery and looked at other human rights issues, I have felt ashamed by what my race has done to other races—just because their skin was a different shade of brown than ours. There's been a lot of talk about whether or not we white Americans—or our country in general—need to make amends for what has happened in the past. I know this is complicated—and this is where some people may believe I'm naive. But I feel a need to apologize on behalf of my ancestors who owned slaves and oppressed people. I don't pretend to know all the answers, and I know a simple apology won't solve the problems. But I still think it's needed and might be one step in moving forward.

As I have worked on this book, I've often been impressed and encouraged by all the great work students are doing to address various social issues. These days almost every youth group is doing some kind of service or missions project—and that's really great. But how many youth groups are working actively to fight racism and build racial and cultural unity while celebrating our differences? I feel that the lack of unity—particularly, the lack of racial unity—is one of our biggest problems, yet I didn't find many student groups actively working to address that issue. With so many problems facing the world today, I'm concerned that we've kind of let the personal and relational problems slip from our priorities.

While researching, I ran across a great article called "The Day Racism Hit Home" by Dara Fisk Ekanger. The article appeared in a Webzine called *Boundless* (www.boundless.org). Ekanger tells the story of a young man of Latin American descent who became close friends with a Caucasian girl in her community. The young guy was well respected in the community and school, but the girl's father was very angered over their friendship—simply because the young man had darker skin than his daughter.

Ekanger talks about how the Bible challenges such racial prejudice:

> *References scattered throughout Scripture confirm God's value of all peoples and desire for integration and harmony. "There is neither Jew nor Greek ... for you are all one ..." (Galatians 3:28). "I looked and saw ... [members] from every nation, tribe, people and language, standing before the throne [of God]" (Revelation 7:9).*
>
> *Forget the "separate but equal" stuff. God intends us to learn from one another, to let the best qualities of peoples and cultures*

rub off on each other. It is idolatry to put one "race" or culture above all others. No matter what an ethnic group or society has accomplished, it cannot truthfully claim to have the corner on all knowledge and wisdom. The Lausanne Covenant eloquently puts it, "Because man is God's creature, some of his culture is rich in beauty and goodness. Because he is fallen, all of it is tainted with sin..."

Ekanger goes on to describe how we are all descendants of Adam. We are all one people. She continues:

It's time for us to acknowledge our imperfections, as individuals and as ethnic groups ... to set aside our pride and with humility get to know people of differently colored skin, ethnicity and background. Those of us who don't experience racism can model acceptance and belief in equality of all peoples. We can stand up for those who are suffering under the unjust prejudices of blind and deceived individuals. But we must guard our own actions and thoughts, lest we become as hate-filled as those we oppose.

It's really easy for me as a white, middle-class American kid to say, "Let's strive for unity" when my people have most often been the oppressors and not the oppressed. I think my people need to make the first move to start cross-racial friendships, and we must recognize that it may take some time to earn trust and respect. We can't expect to overcome racial and cultural boundaries immediately just because our intentions are good. There's often a lack of trust that stems from a whole history of past offenses each person carries into such relationships. So if you try to reach out and there are no breakthroughs—if you're being kept at arm's distance—you have to decide whether you're going to be patient and continue to show love, acceptance, and a desire for true friendship, or whether you're going to cut and run.

> **"Like an unchecked cancer, hate corrodes the personality and eats away its vital unity. Hate destroys a man's sense of values and his objectivity. It causes him to describe the beautiful as ugly and the ugly as beautiful, and to confuse the true with the false and the false with the true."**
>
> Dr. Martin Luther King Jr.

Selfishness and pride are the root causes of many divisions among people. Remember: Unity isn't just racial—it's relational. To break down boundaries, we must build understanding and find common ground. Instead of pointing out where you think someone else is wrong, find something you agree upon and build on that. You don't always have to prove how much you know; sometimes it's better to just listen. My dad often talks about "the power of the question." He says when you're seeking to understand someone else or facing a difficult situation, asking questions and really listening can be a great way to move forward.

IN YOUR SILENCE

I heard about an incident at a Christian high school in which someone had written a racially offensive statement on a hallway wall outside the Bible teacher's classroom. The leadership of the school found out about it, and sent someone to clean it off the wall. But there was never any public discussion about the incident. Perhaps individual teachers addressed the issue with students. But there was no discussion involving the whole student body, no public apology by the administration, and nothing to let the student body know this was completely unacceptable and inconsistent with the teachings of the school.

Perhaps there have been other occasions when the school has expressed a clear commitment to protect students of all races from harassment and offensive speech. But apparently it didn't happen this time. There are very few students at this school who are not white. I think the school missed an opportunity to help create an environment where a more diverse student body could thrive. Instead, they gave the impression that they felt this racist and degrading statement was no big deal—something that could be taken care of easily with some soap and water. We all know that hurtful words just don't go away that easily. Whether it's because of our fears or because we don't want to deal with a difficult issue, sometimes our staying quiet actually sends the wrong message—the message we either condone or aren't disgusted by racism.

I've lived all over the country and I've witnessed racism and divisions in many different forms. Often it's not that people have deliberately excluded others, but more that they allow others to feel unincluded. Friends have held parties and not taken the opportunity to deliberately include someone who is different. People are "friends" in the hallway at school, but they wouldn't invite that "friend" of another race into their home. I know I have stayed silent at times when I should have spoken up.

Even the little comments high school students tend to make—about someone's appearance, or how they act or walk—these things erode unity. When we let this kind of thing go and don't speak up, it becomes acceptable and the cultural norm. Such talk can really get out of hand and can be very damaging to others, their reputations, and their feelings about themselves.

CHANGE IT: MARCH 21

March 21 is the International Day for the Elimination of Racial Discrimination. It commemorates the day protesters were killed in Sharpeville, South Africa, while demonstrating against the country's apartheid policies that discriminated against blacks. Many campuses have chosen this day to hold special events designed to tear down racial stereotypes and to increase appreciation for other cultures. Some hold art exhibits and readings that highlight different cultures. Others hold potluck dinners where each person brings a dish from his or her country of origin, and speakers and musicians provide entertainment. At some high school and college campuses such as Northern Kentucky University, young people have started local chapters of Students Together against Racism (S.T.A.R.) that help organize the special events in March as well as other antiracism activities throughout the year.

Canada holds an annual video competition each year as part of the March 21 campaign against racial discrimination. The "Racism. Stop it!" film competition invites students to submit videos they've produced to raise awareness about racism and help others understand attitudes that lead to discrimination. The ten winning videos are shown on national television. You can learn more at www.pch.gc.ca/march-21-mars//index_e.cfm.

CHANGE IT: YOUR TURN

I want to hear from you. If you're involved in efforts to bring about racial unity, please email me. My contact info is at the end of this book.

BRAINSTORM FOR CHANGE

- Evaluate your own attitudes about people who are different from you. Have you ever failed to invite someone to a party or event because of his or her race? Have you ever thought someone might be dangerous simply because of that person's skin tone? Or, have you assumed someone must be rich, arrogant, or smart because of his or her skin tone? When you go to church, school, the lunchroom, have you ever purposefully chosen to sit with someone who is of a different race? Have you ever had a significant, meaningful conversation with someone from a different cultural background? Get literate about other cultures. The United States is made up of people from many cultures. My own ancestors were German, English, and American Indian. Make an effort to learn about and appreciate your own cultural roots as well as those of your friends.

- Purposefully seek out friendships with people different from you. Be willing to patiently pursue these friendships without expectations.

- Serve on a committee at your school that plans events to increase cross-cultural understanding and honor leaders of other races. Whether it's celebrating Black History Month and the contributions of leaders such as Dr. Martin Luther King Jr. or planning a Latin American or Asian heritage celebration, volunteer and learn.

- Listen closely. Make friends with students who are first-generation Americans and listen to them and their families. Seek to really hear about the adjustments they are making and the challenges they face.

- Invite an immigrant family into your home for a meal. Don't let a potential language barrier get in the way.

- Volunteer at an English as Second Language lab tutoring people trying to learn your language.

- Plan a March 21 event where you learn about other cultures and the struggles of the past.

Corey spent Christmas in a dump in Quito, Ecuador, ministering to children who live there.

CHAPTER 15

FRIENDSHIP

> **"Lots of people want to ride with you in the limo, but what you want is someone who will take the bus with you when the limo breaks down."**
>
> Oprah Winfrey

If you've made it all the way to this chapter, you've probably figured out that my faith is pretty important to me. I think those of us who claim to follow Jesus should learn all we can about how he lived and emulate him. Well, friendship is one of the areas Jesus models well for us.

Being God, Jesus really didn't "need" friends to provide him with anything. But he chose to cultivate relationships and let people get into his life and he got into theirs. He gathered 12 guys to be his closest friends. They traveled together, talked with one another, ate together, challenged one another, and sometimes even got on each other's nerves. Jesus valued these guys as friends, sharing his personal concerns with them and asking them to pray for him when he was at a crisis point.

But Jesus didn't just befriend the "good guys" and the "nice girls"—the popular people. He often sat down to meals with folks whose reputations were not so good. A lot of us hear in church about how "Jesus ate with tax collectors and prostitutes," but I don't think we actually grasp the significance of this in the Hebrew culture at the time. Jesus was basically eating with the lowest of the low, and in that culture (like ours) the people you ate with were the people you were thought to be like. Nobody liked the tax collectors in those days because they worked for the Romans and often ripped people off. And the prostitutes... well, enough said. For Jesus to associate himself with the untouchables of this society was amazing. He not only associated himself with them, but also befriended them, went to their homes, healed them, preached to them, and helped them out. He offered his friendship not just to these people but to all people.

Jesus befriended and surrounded himself with people very different from himself. Of course, anyone would look bad compared with him, but that didn't deter him from connecting with people who needed a friend. If we followed his example, what would the contact list look like in our cell phone? Whom would we sit with at lunch? Whom would we invite to our parties?

Another thing I think is great is the way Jesus responded to the questions the disciples had. For example, in John 16 Jesus says, "In a little while you will see me no more, and then after a little while you will see me." All the disciples were like, "Huh? What does Jesus mean by this?" Jesus tries to explain it to them in a different way, but they are still confused. When he sees they are still not getting it, he finally says, "I came from the father and entered the world; now I am leaving the world and going back to the father" (John 16:28). Then the disciples finally have one of those "Oh!" moments.

> **"Love must be sincere. Hate what is evil; cling to what is good. Be devoted to one another in brotherly love. Honor one another above yourselves."**
>
> Romans 12:9-10

But it was only after Jesus explained himself at least three times, illustrating another great character trait to have as a friend: patience. Jesus never once said, "You guys are sooo dumb! Don't you get it?!" No, Jesus was patient with them.

So how can we apply this? Well, the obvious answer is that we can be more patient in our everyday interactions with people, but how does it apply to a more global level? Maybe when it comes to service work, it means being willing to do the parts that aren't the most fun or that get us the most attention—like picking up trash, or licking the stamps for a mailing, or digging the holes on a building project. None of that sounds like fun. That type of work requires a lot of...patience.

We have all heard the question "What would Jesus do?"—in fact, it's been quoted so often that it's become a cliché. But it's still a question worth asking. What would Jesus do if he were walking the earth today? Would he go around casting out demons, performing miracles, and raising dead people? Maybe. But it's important to remember that his ministry wasn't primarily about doing miracles, it was about people. Jesus demonstrated how we should treat one another through his actions and his parables and his healings. His healings and other miracles were an extension of his love for people. When he healed the sick, he showed us how to treat the disabled and diseased. When he fed the hungry, he modeled compassion and care. When he told the parable of the good Samaritan, he showed us how to treat "our neighbor." And when he died on the cross, he proved he loved the whole unlovely world even to the death.

CHANGE IT: COREY'S STORY

Corey Carnill was born in the States and moved to Quito, Ecuador, when he was four years old. His parents were missionaries who worked with teams that came down to Ecuador to help various ministries. Not long after arriving, Corey and his parents were driving to a small town outside the capital when they noticed a trash dump beside the road. "My parents had visited Guatemala a few years earlier and were very moved by the people they saw living right in the trash at the city dump." When they drove down into the area around the dump, they saw hundreds of people digging through the trash, looking for things to use, eat, and sell. Corey and his family desperately wanted to help the people living in the dump, but the people living there didn't trust strangers. His family knew they'd have to work hard to develop the trust that would allow them to be of help.

They decided to have a community Christmas celebration at the dump that would bring everyone together and show them they were loved. The Carnills told the people at the dump to invite everyone they knew for a big party. That first year more than 300 people came. They gave out shoes, served food, painted the faces of the children, and got to know one another. That was in 1997.

> **"I can remember even as a little boy playing with the kids in the dump. I know their names and they know mine."**
>
> Corey Carnill

Since then the Carnills have continued building relationships with the people who scavenge at the dump and working to improve their lives. Some people might wonder why they don't just "rescue" the people from the dump. The answer is complicated. But for many of the people this is the only life they know. They aren't educated and it would be traumatic to uproot them from all they've known. And it's just not possible to rescue everyone. But it is possible to improve the lives of these families. They've now opened a day care center, a preschool, and a medical clinic for the families living at the dump.

Corey and his family have shown these families consistent friendship in the style of Jesus that's bringing hope for future generations. What started out as a side ministry to the people living at one dump in Ecuador has evolved into Extreme Response, an international organization dedicated to helping those who live in extreme situations and changing their lives.

Corey is 16 now. When I sat down to talk with him recently, I was blown away and really encouraged. He told me, "When you see that people who have nothing can be so happy because they have a simple faith in God, it really makes you think. Many of them are happier than you can ever remember being. You have cars, lots of possessions and privileges, but those things don't bring happiness. I've met many people who are in terrible situations, and God's love just shines through them."

Corey says he continues to be amazed by the way God works in the lives of people who are desperately poor. He spoke of how God is alive in them, "giving them a sense of awe and a love for him and each other. It makes me all the more thankful." He said it makes him feel like he wants to give and do more. (Remember, this is a guy who has lived as a missionary among the poorest of the poor for most of his life.)

Corey told me life isn't always easy in Ecuador, but God always seems to show up. He remembers a time when they were distributing rice to a large group of people. They were almost to the bottom of the barrel and there were still many more people to feed. He remembers them all praying, asking God to help them feed these hungry people. Amazingly, they were able to feed every one of the one hundred or so people with rice that shouldn't have gone anywhere near that far—and they even had some left over.

One of Corey's biggest influences is his dad, who has modeled true friendship with the poor. "My dad has the biggest love for people," Corey says. "Since I was little he wanted me to help with Extreme Response. I can remember even as a little boy playing with the kids in the dump. I know their names and they know mine...and we can just sit down and talk." Sounds like a great way to make friends, huh?

Since he's returned to the States, Corey says he's been reminded many of us just think of ourselves. When I asked him what he'd say to American teens who seem so preoccupied by what they have or don't have, he said, "You have to wake up and open your eyes to the world and see how many people live their lives. Go outside

> **"To be trusted is a greater compliment than being loved."**
> George MacDonald

your comfort zone and experience firsthand what is happening. Think about giving to someone who is less fortunate without receiving anything back. Think about how you can help people move up in life, don't think about how you can move up the social ladder." I think that's what it means to demonstrate true, sacrificial, Jesus-like friendship.

Here's a way you can support the work of Extreme Response and help them bring hope and joy to children living in dumps in the poorest areas in the world: Collect items like toothbrushes, travel-sized toothpaste, small toys, and other small items and send them to Extreme Response. They will package and distribute them to children in the dump at their Christmas in the Dump parties. You can get more information at www.extremeresponse.org.

CHANGE IT: YOUR TURN

Princess Closet

Here's an idea that takes recycling to a whole new level. I'm not sure who started this ingenious project, but it's been done at a number of high schools. You guys may not realize this, but a prom dress can cost as much as $1,000—a price many girls can't afford. Most girls who go to a prom, homecoming dance, or Sadie Hawkins won't wear the same dress to another dance—and most formal dresses aren't something they'd wear anywhere else. So the expensive dress is worn once, then sits in a closet.

Well, girls around the United States have decided to bring those dresses out of hiding and give them a second life. Girls bring in their dresses and they are all displayed in a boutique. The boutique can be set up in a classroom, but shouldn't be run by students or teachers from the school (to prevent embarrassment). Girls who can't afford a brand-new dress can come, try the dresses on, and take home a beautiful dress for free. Some have suggested different schools swap with each other so it's less likely the girl who donated the dress will be at the same dance. Some Princess projects also provide free haircutting and makeup tips. This might seem a little silly to some of us guys, but for some girls this is a great way to be a blessing to others and help someone else's dream come true.

Rosa Loves

Rosa Loves is a grassroots organization that designs and sells T-shirts to meet the personal needs of individual people. When the group learns of a particular person or family in need, they design a specific shirt that illustrates the need in some way, and then print and sell just enough T-shirts to cover the particular situation. Their projects have included providing a walker for a woman who needed it and a boat for a fisherman whose family lives on less than $1 a day.

Rosa Loves wants to connect more-fortunate people with less-fortunate people on a personal and intimate level. Their Web site says, "It's usually thoughts like, 'those people over there' that perpetuate a sense of complacency and lack of concern. Rosa Loves wants to shed light on the stories around us, to give them a real face, a real name."

One family supported by Rosa Loves is the Sharkars, who live in Bangladesh. Mr. Sharkar was a rickshaw driver until he passed away due to a throat tumor. After Mr. Sharkar's death, his 14-year-old son, Babul, took over the job—but because he didn't own the rickshaw, most of the money he made was passed on to the rickshaw owner. Babul and his entire family were extremely malnourished. But with the help of Rosa Loves, Babul now has a new rickshaw, their family has a new home, and Babul's mother has begun raising silkworms again. Rosa Loves also hopes to build a child development center to help the community.

Check out www.rosaloves.org to read the full story of the Sharkars and the many other efforts Rosa Loves is supporting. Maybe you and a group of friends could choose a story there that moves you, buy the shirts available, and use your buying power and clothing choices to change the world! Or, maybe your drama club or youth group could choose a story and perform it for your school or church.

Adopt a Grandparent

Making a friend who is a couple of generations ahead of you will provide benefits to both of you. Our culture often tucks the elderly away somewhere out of sight. I think we're missing out on the great wisdom we can gain from these friends. Here are a couple of ways you can cultivate a friendship with an adopted grandparent:

» Visit a senior citizen center or assisted-living home and just hang out with people and ask them about their lives.

» Hang a wreath on the door of an elderly person and include a kind note.

» Lead a weekly worship service at a senior citizen home.

» Create TLC bags for senior citizens and deliver them to an assisted-living home. Include toothbrushes, slippers, hard candies, a magazine or book, and other items you think someone might enjoy.

BRAINSTORM FOR CHANGE

- Rake the yard or shovel the snow for someone.

- Offer to babysit for a young couple who might not be able to afford a babysitter and could use a night out together.

- Put an anonymous note of encouragement in the locker of someone who has trouble fitting in.

- Sit with someone new at lunch and spend the meal asking questions and listening. Encourage your student council to implement a mix-it-up day, where students deliberately sit with someone new at lunch.

- Buy a package of birthday cards and send them to a missionary family, encouraging them to give them to people on the mission field.

CHAPTER 16

CHANGE BEGINS NOW

> *"For we are God's workmanship, created in Christ Jesus to do good works, which God prepared in advance for us to do."*
>
> Ephesians 2:10

When you got up this morning, people around the world were waiting, maybe desperately dreaming that today might be the day. Today, the day they will finally get relief from their suffering. Today, the day they begin to see hope for their future. Today, the day Jesus comes to their door in the hands and feet of people who care.

Generation Change is not going to wait for someone else—someone who's older or better qualified; someone with more cash or more free time. Generation Change is not going to wait for someday. We are going to seize this day and breathe new life and hope and justice and freedom and peace and love into it. Because, we know that *we are the someone* and *today* is the day!

I'd love to hear more about what you are doing as part of Generation Change. You can contact me directly by email at WeAreGenerationChange@gmail.com. Or you can log on to www.WeAreGenerationChange.org, where you can share your story, offer your own ideas for change, and add the organizations you support. Let's all roll up our sleeves and join together in the movement we hope will change the world.

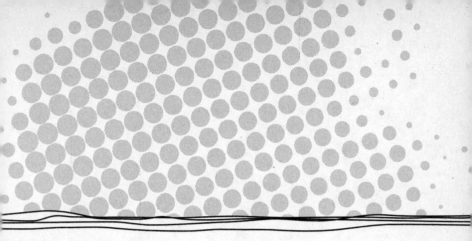

www.WeAreGenerationChange.org

Calendar for Change

Some people think holidays and special days are just another reason for retailers to push greeting cards. Hey, but our generation can reclaim these dates as opportunities to motivate others to create change in the world. You might also want to coordinate some of your activities around these dates. Some of the specific dates change from year to year, so check it out online before you plan anything.

January	Sanctity of Life Day (date varies)
January 1	New Year's Day
January 15	Dr. Martin Luther King Jr. Day
February	Black History Month
February 14	Valentine's Day
March 16	Red Nose Day: Comic Relief to Relieve Poverty

March 20	Earth Day
March 21	End Racism Day
March 22	Water Day
April 24	World Poverty Day
May	National Day of Prayer (date varies)
May	Mother's Day (date varies)
May 10	Fair Trade Day
June	World Refugee Day (date varies)
June	Father's Day (date varies)
July 4	Independence Day
July 17	International Justice Day
August 3	Friendship Day
August 12	Youth Day
August 12	Civil Rights Day
September	Grandparent's Day (date varies)

October 1	Older Person's Day
October 16	End Hunger Day
October 17	End Poverty Day
November	Day of Prayer for the Persecuted Church (date varies)
November 15	Recycling Day
November 20	Children's Day
November	Thanksgiving (date varies)
December 1	World AIDS Day
December 2	International Day for the Abolition of Slavery
December 5	Volunteers Day
December 10	Human Rights Day
December 21	End Homelessness Day
December 25	Christmas

Many people think teenagers aren't capable of much. But Zach Hunter is proving those people wrong. He's only fifteen, but he's working to end slavery in the world—and he's making changes that affect millions of people. Find out how Zach is making a difference and how you can make changes in the things that you see wrong with our world.

Be the Change
Your Guide to Freeing Slaves and Changing the World
Zach Hunter
RETAIL $9.99
ISBN 0-310-27756-6